Success Chronicles:
Networking Marketing Women of Impact

Co-authored by:

Lisa Stubbs

Lisa Wilber

Nora Halko

Melynda Lilly

Alice Hinckley

Amy Jimenez

Dawn Ferrentino

Success Chronicles: Networking Marketing Women of Impact
Copyright © 2018 by UImpact Publishing
All Rights Reserved

No part of this book may be used, reproduced, uploaded, stored or introduced into a retrieval system, or transmitted in any way or by any means (including electronic, mechanical, recording, or otherwise), without the prior written permission of the publisher, with the exception of brief quotations for written reviews or articles. No copying, uploading, or distribution of this book via the Internet is permissible.

The author, writers, and publisher have made every effort to include accurate information and website addresses in this work at the time of publication, and assume no responsibility for changes, omissions, inaccuracies, or errors that occur before or after publication. The publisher does not endorse or assume responsibility for information, author and writer websites, or third-party websites, or their content.

1. Business 2. Internet

ISBN-10: 1720746524
ISBN-13: 978-1720746522
BUSINESS & ECONOMICS: Entrepreneurship

TABLE OF CONTENTS

Lisa Stubbs
-7-

Lisa Wilber
-19-

Nora Halko
-29-

Melynda Lilly
-37-

Alice Hinckley
-57-

Amy Jimenez
-77-

Dawn Ferrentino
-89-

> **No matter what people tell you, words and ideas can change the world. - Robin Williams**

The Success Chronicles: Networking Marketing Women of Impact has dual purposes.

First, to understand the journey, the lessons, hurdles, thought processes, disappointments, triumphs that you go through when building your career and business. Why is it important to learn about other's stories? Although the world is full of people often when you are building a career and business you feel alone and at times you feel you are the only one experiencing the obstacles you face. Hearing and reading the stories of women that you can relate to, can empower you to look at your journey differently.

Second, this book is designed to help you craft your career and business in a way that distinguishes you effectively and memorably in your market. Your audience wants to know how you started your business. How you came to be where you are at this very moment. They want to know what you like to do when you're not pounding the pavement with your brilliant work. They want to know about your path --- they want to know the person behind the brand.

Each of these authors share their obstacles, victories, and offer invaluable information that can help you grow, challenge yourself and look at your situations in a new light. I encourage you to learn from their stories and the lessons they have learned along the way to becoming successful entrepreneurs and professionals.

To Your Impact and Success,
Kimberly Pitts
Founder, UImpact & UImpact Publishing Group

LISA STUBBS

Tell us a little about yourself.

My name is Lisa Stubbs and I am a wife and mother of four (two teenage girls and two young, energetic boys - ages 15, 14, 8 and 6). I grew up in the San Francisco Bay Area and love being Californian with a Texan twist. I graduated from college in Youth Agency Administration under Recreation Management. A year after graduating, I married Sterling Stubbs who grew up in Virginia Beach, VA. He is a regional vice president of an advertising agency here in Dallas. I used my college degree for 9.5 years overseeing summer and after school programs for a school district, as well as being the Volunteer & Jobs for Kids Coordinator. I also received a certification as a National After School Accreditation Endorser and sat on the board for the state School Age Care Alliance.

I took a break from the educational system before our second daughter was born to focus full time on raising children. Now I have found a new passion as a hair consultant with Monat Global, an anti-aging hair care company. I have quickly risen as a Mentor and Founder for Monat. Happy feelings come from spending time with my family and friends, volunteering weekly as an aide for a darling six-year-old Autistic boy, vacationing, exercising, working on living a healthier lifestyle, eliminating toxins from the home (impacted even more due to MTHFR issues), reading, working on self-improvement, and making hair great again...one head at a time.

Share with us how you got started in your business and why you wanted to start this business.

There are three main reasons why I became a business owner. Naturally, I have very thin, fine, limp hair. My hair became very dry and damaged over time. I was even losing gobs of hair in the shower! Of course, I was freaking out. My husband got tired of seeing hair on the shower walls lol. Some of you may know what that feels like. I'd chalked it up to nursing and pregnancies, however when my hair did not look better after that chapter was closed, a stylist recommended that I use Nioxin hair care. When those products were all gone, and they had not improved my situation, I had lab work done and results were normal. An internal medicine doctor recommended a brand of biotin to track progress for months. With no results, she had me switch to another biotin brand for month. After that, I sought out the help from a holistic chiropractor. He had me take multiple supplements for a year and a half. I'm sure they helped my body; however, they did not resolve my hair concerns. I spent several years and numerous dollars on hair treatments. You can imagine how I felt when I learned I could get my money back from Monat if their products didn't work! I had a "risk free" alternative after that wild goose chase. It was a no brainer!

A friend of mine knew about my hair struggles. She'd learned about Monat and added me to a Facebook group called, "MONAT Hair Care – Personal Stories." One night at 11 p.m. I found myself looking at the information before falling asleep. I was enthralled by what I saw! I became mesmerized by reading the testimonies and seeing their AFTER pictures! I wanted my hair to look that beautiful! A few days later, my friend shampooed my hair with the products and I COULD NOT KEEP MY HANDS OUT OF MY HAIR! It was sooo soft and smooth! I went home, started to research where this product was coming from and learned more about the ingredients. At this point in my life, I had started to become very "toxic aware". I'd started realizing what toxins were important to avoid (it only takes 26 seconds for toxins to enter our bloodstream once they touch our skin).

I was thrilled to find out Monat was made in Florida. Another big seller for me was that it is 100% toxin free, and that the family who founded the line was dedicated to family, service and gratitude (things that are very dear to my heart!).

I grabbed a product pack with NO intention of doing a business. I just wanted the greatest amount of product for the best price. I used the products for three weeks and my hair stopped falling out. This meant no more gobs of hair on the shower walls...much to the delight of my husband! After three months, friends started asking me what I'd done to my hair. I realized it was just like when someone loses weight, everyone wants to know what the secret is. After five months of using the products, I finally realized it just made sense to share with others how they could get hair like mine. Never say never, eh?! Besides, I now had my own AFTER picture!

The second reason though is that we had been struggling financially for seven years. We had had fifteen months of double mortgage, then the market took a dive in 2007, and my husband's job felt the impact because ad dollars are usually the first on the chopping block for budget cuts. We lived off a lower salary from his job and dipped every month into our savings using profits from the home sale. It didn't make sense for me to go to work to help pay someone to watch our toddlers in day care. When Monat came into my life, I didn't realize this could be a means to an end. The part time money I was bringing in was exactly what we needed as the money from the sale of the home was almost out! We had made a conscious decision that if we hit a certain low point in our savings that we would put our home on the market and move from Texas to live with my parents in California. Monat made it possible for us to stay put.

The last reason is that before Monat I had allowed myself, as a stay at home mom, to compare myself to others (comparison-itis). This happened because I felt my hair was not-so-pretty. In turn, it affected my self-esteem negatively. Then add the financial burdens on top of that. I allowed the comparison-itis to cause me to be very introverted and it left me with anxiety issues. I had no idea how much my hair insecurity affected how I felt about myself. I know it may sound cliché, however changing my shampoo literally changed my life! I used to mention that He put this opportunity in my lap, however He truly put it in my hair ☺. What a tender mercy. I've learned that so many people have a hair issue or concern.

Monat has been a vehicle for me to not only have beautiful hair again, but it has restored my confidence (and earned me a gorgeous white Cadillac – YES, A HAPPY DANCE INSERTED HERE!!!!). It's such a different feeling to have confidence in oneself, ya know?! I feel alive again, wahoo!! Monat has allowed us more time and financial freedom as a family. My "why" has evolved over time. Now, I am passionate about empowering others to dream again and believe in themselves. Besides, I sincerely want everyone I care about to have better hair care. I love helping others!

What was the biggest obstacle you've encountered? How did you overcome it?

The biggest obstacle I have encountered has been dealing with some negative self-talk. Do any of you ever struggle with that? Sometimes my mind makes up stories that I start to believe that are not true. I personally do not believe it's my mind, but rather Satan trying to get me to quit or give up. I'll be honest- it is a daily battle because we have between 50-70,000 thoughts each day. Thoughts become ideas. We learned from Dr. Bruce Davis that, "the steady flow of thinking is a thick filter between our thoughts and feeling, our head and heart." I have studied a lot and listened when friends have given suggestions. My friend, Ashley, suggested using the Miracle Morning concepts with some of my own additions (like prayer and scripture study). This has made the biggest impact besides my friend, Valoree, assisting me with positive affirmations recorded in my own voice (since we believe our own voice more than anyone else whether it's positive or negative) and listen to it daily.

Nia Peeples taught me last night (yes, from Hollywood), in my friend Cheryl's living room, about the science behind the heart and how the heart is in charge of the brain. So, I'm excited to learn more about implementing 'heart breaths' in my daily practice. Practice makes perfect and helps us remember. It changes our muscle memory or our myelin sheaths and rewires our brains. If you want more on this, head to YouTube and Google Mel Robbins' "5 Second Rule." It's an easy skill that anyone can use to get themselves to change as we all know change can be hard, right?! Anyhow, it takes courage to change and walk into the unknown (things you've never done before). Two of my favorite affirmations are "I'm grateful for my challenges because they help me find my courage," and "What we focus on, we get more of." – Dr. Becky Bailey

What have been your best practices to grow, nurture and retain your client/customer base?

One of the things that I pride myself on and my clients appreciate is that I have not been pushy. It's everyone's choice to participate in Monat, just like it was my choice. I was hesitant to jump into network marketing because sometimes there is a negative stigma. I even had three friends ask me if someone had hijacked my Facebook account when I made my first post about the business. I feel that stigma comes from people who have had to frontload product inventory, so they are desperate to sell it to 'get their money back.' Monat ships direct, so there is no pressure I feel in that regard. It's always fresh product being shipped out. No customer needs to wonder if it's been sitting on the store shelf, or contaminated. I learned recently that we should stand out with our customer service with mailing a hand written thank you note. Expressing appreciation, offering personalized recommendations and advice, providing new product information and hair education have proved beneficial. Like our toxin-free lash & brow growth serum, is a third of the cost of the most popular brand on the market!

Additionally, I have my clients, and those interested in learning more, added to my VIP Facebook group: "Monating Magic – Monat VIP Healthy Hair Group – Tips & Deals." Anyone who is curious about what all the Monat buzz is about is welcome to request to join my group (wink, wink). Thankfully, my company occasionally offers juicy Flash Sales. Last month they offered a chance to earn a

Royal Caribbean cruise and airfare for those who had a qualifying flexship!! I love it when I can help others achieve their hair goals.

What have been your best practices to grow, nurture and retain your team?

I feel it is important to get to know team members individually. We get deep into their "Why" and "Where" do they want to take it. It helps to link arms with them to lead them. Welcome calls facilitate a family feel. I plan weekly calls with them, so they can start to spread their wings. It's kind of like coaching, as I'm not anybody's boss. We are all the CEO of our own business. That's the beauty of it. We can set our own hours. We get paid according to the amount of work we put into our own business.

I notify my team of valuable information or things I feel would be helpful to learn. Their time is precious, just like mine is. Some of us like to host Meet Monats so our new market partners can invite guests to attend and learn more. It's up to the guest on which way they'd like to get involved with Monat (spend, save or make money). I do my best to uplift team members and answer their questions as they come.

I offer incentive challenges and provide raffle gifts. I notice who is most involved on the team page and reward the top 3 with gifts. I have mailed personal development books to those who are working hard. I post accomplishments weekly and monthly for team recognition. I offer training on the team page, encourage team members to attend our corporate trainings, take part in the company's monthly incentives and reach out to those who have goals or need encouragement. Their success is my success. Sr. Luis

Urdaneta, Monat's Founder, said, "If you want to succeed in life, you must first invest in the success of others." Loving on people makes it easier to accomplish this. Can't go wrong with love.

What have been your most successful marketing strategies you have used to grow your business?

Getting involved in networking groups has led me to meet so many amazing people. My life has been so enriched by their friendships. These newfound friendships have led some of them to introduce me to their friends who need the business or products, or both.

Doing Facebook Live videos have been helpful as well. It's an easy tool to pass around to those who need more information about a topic. I am passionate about the benefits of Monat. I have even been approached by strangers who have noticed my social media posts. They've seen my growth over the years. I'm here to tell you that a quiet, anxiety stricken, seemingly overwhelmed mother, can be a confident, passionate, money-making business owner.

What three resources do you feel anyone in network marketing needs? Why?

I feel the three resources anyone in network marketing needs is a personal development book to assist with self-improvement as we need to be the best version of ourselves. Next would be figuring out what the number one thing is that you need to do to produce results. For some it may be learning how to follow up, for others it could be learning how to invite someone to an event. For others it could be how to close a sale. Whichever it might be, that is the one thing they must research, practice and learn so they can improve their skills in business. Work on your weakness. Anyone can learn these skills. The last resource needed would be to have a gratitude journal. This is key to living an abundant life. There is healing power in utilizing the Law of Gratitude.

How do you keep yourself motivated and encouraged when things don't go right?

Let's be real. There are hard days. There are days that don't go as planned. And that's okay! Nurturing my mindset has helped me to not sweat the small stuff. Life happens. Laughing at myself also lightens stress levels. Knowing my "why" is important because my "why" is stronger than any fear that I have. Thomas Edison failed many times while working toward his light bulb invention. Remember the great Michael Jordan was cut from his junior high basketball team. Henry Ford, Philo Farnsworth, Carrie Underwood and Steve Jobs all worked hard toward achieving their visions. Success did not happen overnight. We must fail forward. We must get up when we fall, just like a toddler learning to walk. It's important to keep walking one step after the next, always pushing ahead, even if those steps seem to be going up a mountain. It's worth it!

What advice would you give to a woman entrepreneur who is ready to take her business to the next level?

First, one must be willing to dream. Then we must believe we can do it, even if it's simply acting on a little bit of faith. Faith requires action. The next step is to achieve, or to take action steps from a plan. We must know where we want to go before we can make the first move otherwise we'll wind up wherever or better yet nowhere. We need to be intentional, set goals and figure out how to make those goals become small and simple steps. Then you follow that road map consistently. By small and simple things are great things brought to pass.

The Chinese Bamboo watering process takes four to five years and then in just six weeks, it spouts 90 feet tall. It really took 5 years for this growth, with consistent nurturing and watering. It's just like a garden. We plant seeds, nurture the garden and then the harvest comes.

I run across a lot of women and I find the successful women to be those who are happy, grateful, passionate, have a work ethic, have a vision and focus on the positive. They attract success. Never give up and always believe in yourself. Anything is possible if you put your mind to it. Look to Him for guidance and offer prayers of gratitude when His blessings come. And just go for it!

What are your insights about the direct selling/network marketing industry that will help women growing their own independent consultant business?

Focus on your hopes and dreams and not somebody else's. Find a product that works well and that you can be passionate about. Start organizing yourself right away. Keep track of your expenditures. Learn to time block. Know what your priorities are and keep them in alignment. Set parameters to balance your life. Set goals because that is what successful people do. Less than 10% of the population sets goals, let alone achieves them. Reading personal development books is a MUST!

What book(s) would you recommend to women starting their own business?

- The Energy Bus by Jon Gordon (positive energy, helps with everyday life too)
- GoPro by Eric Worre (eight skills to learn)
- Get Over Your *$%# Self by Romi Neustadt (blueprint for getting the business started)
- It Matters by Kimberly Pitts (workbook to challenge yourself)

Learn more about Lisa Subbs

Lisa Stubbs, first and foremost is a daughter of God, wife to Sterling of 19 years heading toward eternity, and mother of 4 beautiful children. Her lifelong passion has been to help others, especially women feel beautiful inside and out. Lisa's love for others started at a young age by volunteering at religious youth camps and has continued into her career, working with educational programs for nearly a decade. Now in the beauty industry, Lisa is a USA Founder/Mentor of Monat Global's anti-aging/toxin free hair care products, which have become the #1 premium hair care brand in America.

LISA WILBER

Tell us a little about yourself.

My name is Lisa Wilber, but most of my colleagues call me "Captain Platinum" these days. I'm a mom, daughter, and a lot of other things, including an Avon business owner. You know, an "Avon Lady!" I prefer to call myself an entrepreneur as I truly enjoy trying to find ways to capitalize on every earning opportunity. My primary job is being a mom, though, and I take that very seriously. I adopted my daughter, Lydia, as a newborn when I was 42 years old. Being single, one of the best features of my business is the flexibility. I am home in the morning to put Lydia on the bus, and home at night when she returns. Soccer game? No problem, I can go! And the ever-growing income from my direct sales business makes it easy to say "yes" to the extra things that make childhood fun. Can you attend Horse riding girl scout camp for two weeks? Yes, you can! Can we see a Broadway show as a Christmas present? Yes, we can! Our life has been full of adventure and blessings thanks to the income from my business.

Share with us how you got started in your business and why you wanted to start this business.

I signed up to sell Avon in 1981 at the age of 18 (don't do the math) when I found myself in Guam married to a sailor and wanting money of my own. I worked various jobs since I was about 12; babysitting, waitressing, working in tobacco fields, office work, etc.

I was used to having my own money. I saw some of the other wives doing party plan companies such as Tupperware and Princess House, but I didn't see anyone doing Avon. I remembered the Avon Lady that came to our house when I was a young girl. My first pierced earrings were from Avon, and my first perfume was Sweet Honesty. Since I didn't see anyone selling Avon, I wrote to the company in the U.S. and asked them if I could sign up to sell in Guam. They said that all I had to do was send them $35 and I could get a starter kit and be an Avon Lady, so that's what I did! I sold the two and half years that I lived in Guam and did quite well, achieving their sales level of "President's Club" in my first year.

Getting married at a young age was a bad idea, as you might have guessed, so when the marriage ended, I moved to Mississippi. (I didn't want to move back home with my parents and hear "I told you so.") I lived in Mississippi for a couple years and sold Avon part time; then, I moved to South Carolina for a year and sold Avon there as well. My Avon business was always a part-time extra income thing for me then; I never thought of it as a full-time possibility. My last big move was to New Hampshire in 1985. Although I had worked low-paying jobs in Mississippi and South Carolina, I applied for a secretarial job in New Hampshire, and was hired! At the time, I thought it was my big break: Full-time income, benefits including medical and dental, retirement savings. I went from making $6,000 per year at a convenience store in South Carolina to earning $15,000 per year plus benefits as a secretary. A little more than two years in to my great new job, the pay increased so that I was making $20,000 per year! But then, our whole department got laid off in the recession of 1987. Right before Thanksgiving. I was devastated. I was married to husband number two by then, and he was never big on earning money, so it was my income we relied upon. When I came home after receiving the news about the layoffs, he asked, "Why don't you do more with that Avon thing you've been playing with?" I thought, *You are kidding, right?* I answered, "I don't know anyone making full-time money doing Avon!" He replied, "Why does that matter? Just because you don't know anyone doing it, why couldn't you be the one who does?" I thought, *Wow! He must really believe in me to say that!* and I built my business with that confidence. Later, he told me, "I didn't mean that I believed in you, I just wanted to say something that would get you to stop crying!" By the time he told me that, it was okay. I thought he believed in me long enough for me to believe in myself.

What was the biggest obstacle you've encountered? How did you overcome it?

My biggest obstacle was and continues to be **me**. I've never had an abundance of self-esteem. But, one thing I *have* always had is a strong desire to not be poor. As my income has grown, it's been a constant battle to keep learning and growing so that I feel worthy of the pay, or I find myself sabotaging my success. I find myself constantly seeking new books, audio programs, and classes on all aspects of my business, as well as personal development to ensure that I continue to grow myself along with my income.

What have been your best practices to grow, nurture, and retain your client/customer base?

I believe that connecting with my customers and including them in my business has helped it tremendously. For example: when my company offered a cruise for being a top seller, I enlisted my customers' help and gave them all kinds of information about the trip. I wore a flower lei around my neck to get people to ask me about it. I carried a big thermometer with me to show the amount of sales I needed to earn the trip, and I showed every customer my progress and how they helped it. Once I earned the cruise, I came back and shared my excitement about how the trip went and showed them my trophy and souvenirs. I thanked them and made sure they knew they made it possible. The customers feel ownership of the trips (I've earned over thirty-five), and now they say things like, "Where are we going this year?" as if they are going with me. We work on it together.

What have been your best practices to grow, nurture, and retain your team?

My entire team gets a "basic level of service" which includes e-letters, access to bi-weekly livestream training, birthday cards, company anniversary certificates, welcome packs, and access to our Team Facebook group page for ongoing support and involvement. Top producers (both in sales and team building) get more: a gift along with their birthday card (the size of the gift is determined by the level of their sales), award certificates for sales and team performance, and much more personalized attention. I have a large team, and I try to see how many of my members I can "touch" each day in a meaningful way for them, whether that be by text, phone call, note in the mail, Facebook private message, or public recognition.

What have been your most successful marketing strategies you have used to grow your business?

I think it's important to realize that with marketing, one needs to do many things all at once. "Trying one thing" or "finding the best way" will lead to limited success, in my opinion. I once read a quote that said anyone could be successful if enough people knew who they were and what they did. I have used that strategy throughout my direct sales experience. I wake up each morning with the thought: *How can I get myself, my products, and my company's opportunity in front of more people today?* Some of the things that I do include: having an advertising wrap on my car including a light-up sign on the roof, I've joined the local Chamber of Commerce, I have a sign on my front lawn, I always wear a name badge or company promotional button, I run classified line ads in local newspapers, I sponsor a sports team, I've run for public office, I have joined a women's networking organization, I place posters on bulletin boards, and I give three business cards to each person I meet and say, "One for you, and two for two of your friends."

What three resources do you feel anyone in network marketing needs? Why?

Two of the best resources that I use in my Avon business also happen to be network marketing companies: SendOutCards, and the Shuffle virtual business card phone application. I have used SendOutCards for about nine years for recruiting and supporting my Avon team. It has been indispensable! From the time I began to use SendOutCards, I have sent out over 43,200 cards! I find it so valuable, because I can design and personalize the cards and then delegate the task of sending them. It gives the receiver the experience of getting something personally from me, but I can have someone else do the day-to-day task of sending them. It's affordable, even for new users. I would use the service for any type of company. I can't imagine that I would have been able to provide the level of service that I have over all these years without it.

The Shuffle virtual business card app for my phone is a relatively new addition; I was just introduced to it in May of 2017. The reason I find it so valuable is the ease and ability to use it, as well as the many uses for it. It's like a personalized website that also has links to my sign-up page and my online store, as well as any links to YouTube videos or social media sites that I want to add. I can text it to prospects as well as new team members, customizing it for each. I also have been using it extensively to follow up with old prospects that never signed up from years past. The technology is fabulous!

My third resource would have to be Facebook groups. I have a Facebook group page with 2,000 of my 8,000 team members on it, and we are building that percentage all the time. I can connect with them more easily and share ideas quicker. I post recognition every two weeks, and they can interact with me and the other team members, so there is a better sense of community. I can also livestream right from my group page and have team members join in as well as ask questions live. Because Facebook archives the videos in the group, new team members have a ready source of training and inspiration from the beginning.

How do you keep yourself motivated and encouraged when things don't go right?

I have close friendships with colleagues in my company who are not in my downline (or upline). We can talk to one another and share frustrations and talk strategy in ways that would be inappropriate if they were on my team. For example: we can blow off steam with each other about a change in the compensation plan or a product introduction we don't like-something I would never discuss with my team. We plan get-togethers that we call "Mastermind Weekends" where we hang out together and exchange ideas, but mainly blow off steam and have fun. Another strategy I use to stay motivated is read affirmation cards with "I am" statements written on them. I read my cards in the morning, and before I go to bed at night. I also have a song playlist that I listen to when I am feeling challenged or depressed about how things are going.

What advice would you give to a woman entrepreneur who is ready to take her business to the next level?

Make sure you are prepared for the long haul. In my experience, earning a six-figure income annually requires persistent, consistent work over a long period of time. You have to believe you are going to be successful despite what everyone is saying around you. You have to be willing to adapt to changes that come in many forms, including: compensation plan changes, changes in company management, changes in the economy, and changes in your team and customer base. The biggest asset in your business is going to be your time, which many people don't count. The ability to delegate all tasks that can be done for less than what you are worth is a major skill that frees you up to concentrate on business-building and finding new customers and team members.

What are your insights about the direct-selling/network marketing industry that will help women who are growing their own independent consultant businesses?

Our profession (direct sales/network marketing) is so diverse that just about every woman could certainly find a company that they could get excited about. Just about every product available can be found in our industry, and I honestly don't believe you need to be a "salesman" type of person to succeed. This business is about relationships and connecting with people. It's about letting people know what you do and being of service. It's about providing information and being available. My best advice is: choose a company you can be passionate about and stick with them. I've been with the same company for over thirty-five years! It would have been easy to company hop every time I saw a better opportunity, but I'm very glad that I stuck it out. There will be ups and downs with every opportunity. Treat it like a real business, and it will pay you like a real business; treat it like a hobby, and it will cost you like a hobby.

What book(s) would you recommend to women starting their own businesses?

One of my all time favorite books is **The Success Principles** by Jack Canfield. I also think everyone should listen to the audio program **Lead the Field** by Earl Nightingale. A YouTube video that I watch over and over is *You Gotta Be Hungry*, presented by Les Brown at a stadium. Powerful!

Learn more about Lisa Wilber

Lisa Wilber is one of six Platinum Executive Leaders with Avon in the United States and has been selling products and building a team since 1981. She is currently the number five money earner in the U.S. business with 9 generations of team members that cover every state in the Union totaling just shy of 8,000 active Representatives.

Referred to by Avon as the "Best Known Representative in the World", Lisa's story has appeared in magazines such as "Fortune", "Networking Times", "Empowering Women" and "Avon Dreams". Lisa Wilber made the list of "The 50 Most Influential People in Direct Sales" issued by www.directsellinglive.com three years running and in 2007 was named Avon's "Woman of Enterprise", the top award given to non-employees. She was the 2013 Avon "Yellow Rose of Courage" recipient.

Lisa was named the 2015 Top Female MLM Networker in the world by Business For Home web site and awarded the "People's Choice Award" at the 2017 Ambitious Women Conference. She has been a professional member of the National Speakers Association since 1998 and has conducted trainings worldwide. She is the author of three books and the co-author of nearly a dozen more. Currently she is the Project Leader for a book series entitled "A View from the Top" featuring chapters written by 63 of Avon's top leaders in a three book and audio series.

You can reach her by e-mail: LWilber@aol.com or on her Facebook business page: www.Facebook.com/winnerinyou.
To purchase Avon from Lisa: www.NHLipstickLady.com

NORA HALKO

Share with us how you got started in your business and why you wanted to start this business.

The "why" is the most important information you need to start any business-whether it is with a direct-selling company or starting your own company. The "why" will also come up because it is the driving force behind your business. The obvious answer is *more money*, right? Of course, you want to increase your income, but your "why" is more than just about money. For example, in my future, I know my husband Shaun and I are going to start a family. The question then arises: How am I going to raise and support my family? Being home with my children-especially in the first few years-is extremely important to me. I need flexibility to work when and how much I want to. When the time comes that I become the "stay at home mom," I will be extremely blessed. I know that being a mother will fulfill my life more than I can understand, but there will always be this other part of me: the working woman and the entrepreneur spirit that I will need to fill as well. It is important to have something of your own that you have built. It builds a more secure life for you, your children, and your family. The "what ifs" in life are there to make us mindful of our steps, but not to cripple our spirit.

Even though it has all the structures I need in life, there is another major reason for joining the direct-selling world. When my husband Shaun and I moved to Texas and I began working in management for another coffee company, I loved it! It was a lot of work and long days, but I felt like I was making a difference. During my first year with this company, I was moved around from store to store several times to help with openings or just to help stabilize a store and make it more successful. In my last year of management with them, I felt confined to do certain things, and those things had to be done in a certain way. The best way I can describe it is: They wanted a square, and I was a triangle. The more I tried to be the square for them, the worse it got, and I felt ever more pressure to become a square. I could not be myself or do the things I thought were in the best interest of the people who worked for me. I decided it was probably best to find a new path, so I found a 9-to-5 job with really no leadership requirements. A little after a year, I realized I truly missed being a leader and helping others to succeed. Starting the business I did enabled me to be a part of a team as well as build a new one and truly help others create a happy and secure life.

What was the biggest obstacle you've encountered? How did you overcome it?

Starting a business always comes with unforeseen circumstances or obstacles. The number one obstacle for me was developing the ability to push past my comfort zone. It terrified me to put myself out there on social media and open myself and my life to the world. The very first Facebook and Instagram live posts I made, I was extremely nervous. Stressed myself about it the whole day. What was I going to say? How was I going to say it? What order was I going to say it in? When the time came, I was almost too tired to even do the live chat. Being shy and introverted, I have to work hard to push past those boundaries. This is an ongoing struggle; anytime an opportunity presents itself and I feel it will push me out of my comfort zone, I know it is something I must do. I will typically give the opportunity some great thought instead of just letting it pass me by. Always push yourself to do things you haven't done before. If it does not work out, learn from it. If it does, then build on it. Strength and knowledge come not only from success stories, but failures as well.

What have been your best practices to grow, nurture, and retain your client/customer base?

The best practice is to listen to what the customer needs and wants. The nice part of selling Monat is there is something for everyone. There is no need to push something that the customer does not want or need. Give them your full attention and follow up without being pushy. I have lost count of how many times a sales person has been just a little too pushy (and I know you have, too). It was an automatic turn off right? When the subject of Monat is brought up, I am enthusiastic and upbeat about the product, but I give them the space to make the decision that's best for them. I want the customers to feel comfortable coming to me, instead of running away.

What have been your most successful marketing strategies you have used to grow your business?

Marketing strategies that have been successful for me thus far are simple. I have been sharing myself and my story. Scary, right? Using social media and being me and showing the product in action has garnered the best response yet. Every part of my being is telling me to safeguard myself and not put myself out there. But every time that I have, there has been a positive response. I believe if people see the true and real you, they will see you as being more genuine than just someone trying to sell a product. The other strategy is allowing my customers to use the products before ever committing to anything. Very rarely does someone not want a free sample, most of the time they will take one. Once they have tried it, I ask them to let me know what they thought. After reconnecting with them and seeing how the samples worked for them, I will then talk about the business and buying options.

What three resources do you feel anyone in network marketing needs? Why?

The number one resource is a daily, weekly, and monthly planner-whether it is an app or a physical planner. Time management is extremely important to keep everything in order to maximize time and effort. The second resource would be a money and expense management tool. No matter what level or size your business is, this is important to keep track of all inputs and outputs. I also use various apps to help build unique and creative social media posts, such as Layout and Typorama. There are many out there-you just need to find the one that works best for you. These are easy and inexpensive tools that can give your business a creative and more appealing look.

How do you keep yourself motivated and encouraged when things don't go right?

Every day is a new day with new opportunities. I know, sounds so cliché, right? But it is true, and only if you let yourself be open to the opportunities will you see a real difference. Over the years, people have told me to wake up and read motivational quotes or imagine what I want my life to look like. At first, I thought: *This is silly. How is imagining things ever going to change anything?* But I started waking up and doing something positive-whether it was looking up motivational quotes on Pinterest, reading my devotional, or just imagining how I wanted my life (or even my day) to go. It truly put me in a positive mindset to start the day. I tell ya, the days I do not do this, my positive mindset and attitude is not there. Also there are days I do get discouraged, especially now that I'm just starting my business. Keeping a positive mindset and kicking the negative thoughts to the curb keeps me going. When things get really tough, I will go back to my why and remember the reasons I am here and what I want to accomplish.

What advice would you give to a woman entrepreneur who is ready to take her business to the next level?

Alright, ladies, you want to go to the next level? Well, first you need ask yourself: *What is the next level? Why do you want to achieve this next level, and what will this bring?* Several times throughout my managing career, I would have employees come up to me and say, "I want to be a shift supervisor/assistant manager." The first question I would ask them is why? Typically, I would get the usual "to make more money" response. Then I would ask, "Does wanting more money make you a great leader?" I would get the "deer-in-headlights" look. Work on what will make you successful at that next level-not just what it takes to get there. Really learn what the next level will require, and build yourself to meet *and exceed* those requirements. Whenever I was trying to move up into a higher position or do something different, I would go to someone in that position and ask them questions. I would strive to be better than the day before and recognize my shortcomings and focus on strengthening those weak spots. Then I'd just go for it! Do not let anyone tell you that you cannot do it. If I had listened to all the people who did not think I had it in me, I would not have gotten where I am today.

What are your insights about the direct-selling/network marketing industry that will help women who are growing their own independent consultant businesses?

KEEP GOING! I am not going to lie, there are days where I wonder if it is all worth it. I am probably not supposed to say that, but it is true. Do not get caught up in comparison and see others' success in the business and think, "Why am I not at that level?" Most likely that person has worked for years developing her business or strategies that work for her. Give yourself a break and keep learning, exploring, and pushing yourself every day. Also, be humble when success does come, and help others just as people have helped you.

What book(s) would you recommend to women who are starting their own businesses?

Over the years, I have read several books on management and leadership. The two books I have been dipping my toes into are **Get Over Your Damn Self** by Romi Neustadt, and **Girl Code** by Cara Alwill Leyba. **Get Over Your Damn Self** has a no-nonsense vibe, and speaks directly to building a successful business. **Girl Code** is a look at building oneself to be able to build a successful business. I especially like the space at the end of each chapter for notes and thoughts. Really helps to reflect on yourself and the information you have just received. I cannot wait to look back five years from now and see if I have the same goals and visions. But there are many books out there about starting your own business and it is up to you to learn whether the strategies suggested will work for you or not.

Learn more about Nora Halko

My name is Nora Halko and you can say I am your typical woman trying to find her path. The path being with my family and finding a career that I love and I'm passionate about. I am married to a wonderful and always supporting husband Shaun. We have four dogs, two cats, two goats and one old horse. Needless to say, our house can be a little nutty at times. I am a shy introvert, who will always observe over speaking. I guess you can say I am your typical country girl. I was fortunate to grow up on 160 acres just north of a national park, you may have heard of it Yellowstone National Park? Growing up in the country with my Dad taught me so many valuable lessons. The very first lesson was to work hard and to never give up. The country life style also taught me to have compassion for animals and other people. Growing up I always wanted to live in a big city and now that I am thirty I would not trade the country life for anything. I love living in Texas and getting to meet so many great people, but the mountains will always be my home.

My journey to direct sales and being a part of the Monat family is something I never thought I would do. I started my business career as a manager in the coffee industry. Being a Barista was my first "real job" and did not take me very long to work up in to leadership roles and management. I love to have challenges and to help grow businesses and people. This is just me and my side of things and I hope it will help or encourage you in whatever endeavor you are on.

MELYNDA LILLY

Tell us a little about yourself.

I am happy to have been married to my high school sweetheart, Mark Lilly, for thirty-seven years. So, you can say we truly both grew up together and I would not change a thing. This man has treated me like a princess our entire married life. I thank God daily for this match made in heaven. We are blessed to have three grown children Keith, Krista, and Chad. Truly amazed to have eight grandchildren: Gavyn, Ethan, Landon, Chase, Taylor, Peyton, Briar and Violet. We are truly grateful and blessed these little angels call us Nana & Papa.

Our life revolves around our family. We spend most of our time attending grandkids sporting events including baseball, football, volleyball, basketball, cheerleading, & gymnastics. We love attending all their events and being their biggest cheerleaders. Our family loves the outdoors; we love to spend as much time as possible on the water. We have a lake house where we spend 90% of our time. The grandkids love to come and stay. They spend most of their time outdoors, riding the golf cart, or hanging out in the hot tub listening to music. The kids love to fish in the pond stocked with catfish. Of course, in the summer you will find us on the lake pulling the grand kids tubing & wake boarding. I love just to float and relax and enjoy the beautiful sunsets. We call our lake house the Lilly Pad. I too enjoy relaxing in the hot tub with a glass of red wine, counting my many blessings of this incredible life we get to live. We also love to travel with family and friends to see the beaches of the world. I love making unforgettable memories with my family & friends at the lake. We love to have family & friends come and stay a few days to enjoy our home, just sitting on the back deck listening to the birds, enjoying our beautiful view or relaxing in the hot tub.

I am truly a people person. I love meeting new people and building relationships with people from all walks of life. There is always a reason to celebrate life! My daughter Krista and I are always planning a birthday celebration, anniversary celebration, holiday parties, etc. You name it, and we will plan a party for it. Life is a celebration!

I love to read motivational books and attend personal growth and development seminars. I was very blessed to have a great coach and mentor. She taught me that when the student is ready the teacher will appear. So, at the young age of 26, I became an avid student of personal growth and development. I have attended many seminars with Jim Rohn, Tony Robbins, Tom Hopkins, John Maxwell, Zig Ziglar, Darren Hardy, Eric Worre, Caterina Rando, DeDe Murcer Moffett, Sandra Yancey, Esther Spina, Jan Ruhe, Jack Canfield and many others. I thank them all for the wisdom they poured into their trainings and books. My life has been forever changed because of them. The best advice I can give is to never, ever stop learning; continue your journey of personal growth and development for a lifetime.

I am truly blessed with exceptional parents, Charlotte & Rex Powell, who role modeled unconditional love. My dad was also an entrepreneur; he owned and operated a machine shop. The things that made my dad successful, he passed down to his family. Let me share these helpful insights with you.

#1 You must be a survivor. Things won't always be easy but will be worth it! My dad would always say, "Where there is a will there is a way!"

#2 You must be driven! Never let your past determine your future.

#3 You must have a strong work ethic.

#4 You must be a fighter. Never give in or give up! Go for your dreams!

#5 Family is everything! My dad worked hard to leave a legacy for his family for generations to come. My dad always told me, "If you are going to work hard you might as well work hard for yourself."

I am glad I followed in his footsteps and can help others do the same. My mom is amazing and my best friend. Our lake house is right next door to her house. We bought the lake house right after my dad passed away almost 3 years ago. So, I am truly blessed to be able to be there for my mother. We play cards, enjoy the hot tub, and enjoy all our meals together. I have been truly blessed to have great role models in my parents.

God truly blessed me when he brought me the man of my dreams, Mark Lilly. We were high school sweethearts. We started dating my sophomore year in high school. I graduated high school in May 1981, and we got married June 6th, 1981.

Our life has truly been a fairy tale! He is the most amazing caretaker; always putting others needs before his own. He continues to be very involved in our kid's lives and super involved in our grandkids lives.

Mark was diagnosed with MS at the very young age of 34. I have watched him deal with his disease over the years. What I have learned from Mark's attitude is to never give in or give up. Most people would never know Mark had MS because he never complains and always pushes through to attend everything he can that deals with family and friends. Mark is my biggest supporter and cheers me on in everything I do. The stress of not having to worry about money because of my Network Marketing business is a significant burden off of him. Our motto is to live each day like it is your last! Live life with no regrets, attend everything, and make time for what's important. We love making unforgettable memories together with our family, friends and business partners.

Share with us how you got started in your business and why you wanted to start this business.

It was my lucky day to have received a phone call on January 2, 2007. Nancy Cotton had gotten involved with Ambit Energy and was working with David Spina. I knew Nancy from my previous MLM business. I had done fundraisers at her hospital for their child care facility for the past ten years. So of course, I thought she was calling me to schedule their fundraisers for the year.

Nancy and David made that three-way call to ask me if I would consider taking a look at Ambit Energy and give them my opinion about the opportunity since I had experience in network marketing. I said, "Of course I would be happy to look at your website and will give you my feedback." David Spina continued to follow back up with me for the next three weeks.

I was curious how they were doing an MLM business with energy deregulation. David asked me if I would do him a favor and let him take me to lunch, and to meet the owners of Ambit and see the operation. He said, "I promise if it is not for you, I will not call you again." So, I thought why not, going to get a FREE lunch. I was kind of curious as to how this all worked. So, David came to my house and picked me up and took me to lunch, where I also met his mother, Esther Spina.

After lunch, we went over to the Ambit Energy home office, where I met Jere Thompson Jr. & Chris Chambless. Chris explained the Ambit compensation plan on a whiteboard. I thought WOW there is a lot of money to be made with energy deregulation. I got very excited about the possibility. I thought well this should be easy, everyone uses electricity, and they buy it every single month. Plus, I was very impressed with Jere Thompson Jr. & Chris Chambless. I liked them both from that first impression; they were both so down to earth and friendly.

I came home and told my husband, "Guess what? You know that energy company I said I was not going to do? Well, I am doing it. I met the owners, and I have no doubt these men are going to build a billion-dollar business, and I don't want to miss the boat!" So, I became happily enrolled as an independent energy consultant on January 31st, 2007. The best decision I have ever made.

I thank my lucky stars David Spina was persistent and continued to follow up with me for three weeks. He would leave messages every week to see if I had looked at their website. Of course, the answer was NO I had not. I was busy working my own MLM business, keeping my grandkids and doing some marketing part time for my chiropractor--my plate was full.

The key lesson here is the fortune is in the follow-up! Pick up your prospects and offer to buy them lunch or dinner and take them to the presentation. When I was invited to become a business partner with Ambit Energy, the concept of no inventory, no deliveries, and no collections greatly appealed to me. Once I enrolled with Ambit Energy every month when my customers paid their electric bill, I get paid a portion of that bill creating a residual income. I get paid month after month after month. I loved the fact that I help people save money on a bill they must pay every month. I have helped hundreds of people eliminate their electric bill with Ambit's FREE energy program.

Because Ambit is a family business, I leave a legacy to my grandchildren and future grandchildren for generations to come. My business is a generational wealth building business, and that makes me happy! 99.9% of my time is invested in helping people make money with Ambit Energy. I love changing a person's financial future for the better.

My reason for starting this business is simple: to help average people earn an above average income, so they can do things in their life they are passionate about! I love the fact that I don't sell a product. I don't have to convince anyone to try my products or try to fit it into their monthly budget. Everyone has already budgeted for their electricity bill. I just help them lower that bill or even get it for free.

Since I had already been involved in the direct selling industry for over 20 years, I was a believer in network marketing. I loved the benefits network marketing had to offer. You are your own boss, the tax advantages, flexible hours, minimum investment, unlimited income potential; you are an independent contractor with residual income.

I knew energy deregulation would be a fast-growing industry, and it was just getting started. I knew if I worked 10 to 15 years in this business, I would be leaving a legacy for my family. When I started with Ambit, I was committed to building this business for as long as it took. There is a day you get into network marketing, but nothing happens until network marketing gets into you. For the first two years, I worked Ambit alongside with my other businesses. Ambit Energy did become a billion-dollar company in 7 years with over 1 million customers. I am very grateful that I made the decision to start my own Ambit Energy business.

My desire is to mentor, inspire and empower other men and women. I have been truly blessed to have some great mentors and teachers in my life. They believed in me and taught me to work harder on myself to develop the skills I needed to build a business. I am honored to pay it forward to help others be the best they can be and live the life they deserve. When I can make a difference in someone's life for the better, then I know it will impact the world because they can go out and do the same for someone else.

What was the biggest obstacle you've encountered? How did you overcome it?

- Avoid Negative people! Surround yourself with positive people!
- Quit focusing on your failures, instead focus on your success.
- Quit being the victim and take full responsibility for creating the life you want.

"If you are an average person with a negative attitude, you are halfway to the bottom. If you are an average person with a positive attitude, you are half way to the top." Roger Crawford

Learning to work with people who deserve my time, not the people who need it. I desperately wanted people to be successful. I would go out of my way to help them, but they would always have excuses why they could not do something. I have learned to say at the very beginning with a new team member, "My efforts will match your efforts. I will work as hard for you in your business as you are willing to work yourself." Now I do not feel guilty if the person is not successful because they did not put any effort into their business. You can make a million excuses, or you can make a million dollars. Your choice!

One of my biggest obstacles is time management. I still work on this every day. It's easy to get caught up in busy work, emails, social media, etc. One of the things that have helped me is an activity tracking worksheet. This has helped me to track my activity for the week. Also, I learned from Dr. John Maxwell to have a Rule of 5. This is five things that you work on every day in your business.

My Rule of 5:

1. Every day I expand my list
2. Every day I invite
3. Every day I learn
4. Every day I encourage
5. Every day I give thanks

Get an accountability partner and have weekly calls to talk about what you did accomplish from the previous week and discuss your action plan for the current week. Having weekly goals all written out and being able to check them off during the week will help you stay focused. I know it did for me!

I also set 30-day goals each month for my personal goals and team goals. You MUST write those goals down and be looking at them daily.

What have been your best practices to grow nurture and retain your client/customer base?

Loyal customers are the bread and butter for any business. It's much easier to take care of the customers you have vs. continually searching for new ones.

- I send out hand written thank you notes to all my customers, thanking them for their business.
- I will reward my customers at Thanksgiving, Christmas, and New Years sending out gift cards thanking them for being a loyal customer.
- Excellent customer service is key!

- Always return phone calls promptly!
- Be accessible! My customers know they can call me anytime if they have a need and I will do my best to take care of it.
- My motto has always been the customer is always right! No matter what!
- Be upbeat and friendly. Shower your customers with Kindness!
- People do business with people they know like and trust! Make sure your customers know they can trust you to take care of them.
- Don't neglect existing customers. I will call, text or email reminding them of their renewal dates.
- Smile, Smile, Smile! Your customers can feel that energy on the phone or in person!

What have been your Best practices to grow nurture and retain your team?

People don't care how much you know until they know how much you care!

1) Find out what people want first, and then show them how to get what they want.
2) Ask Questions to get to know your consultants. Ask Questions about their family, their occupation, what they like to do for Fun, etc.
3) Recognition is KEY! You can never recognize your leaders enough!
4) Pick up the phone and call your TEAM!

5) Personal hand-written cards
6) Promotion parties with your team! Celebrate all rank promotions.
7) Have a cook out for no reason at all but just to connect with your team.
8) Corporate conventions get a suite; host a cocktail party for your team.
9) Train the Trainers! You must duplicate!
10) Teach your Team Personal Growth and Development!

This is the biggest secret to success! Once people start working on themselves, they build their confidence and watch them soar!

What have been your most successful marketing strategies you have used to grow your business?

You must always be prospecting! I consider myself a master networker because I connect with people from all walks of life anytime anywhere. Doctor office, grocery store, parks, networking events, seminars, kids sporting events, restaurants etc etc. It's called the 3 ft rule. Anyone within 3 ft of me is a prospect. No, I am not talking to them about my opportunity at that time but just making a connection to build a relationship. So excited last year I started using a digital business card that is a game changer for prospecting. Plus is a great conversation starter, especially if the person you are chatting with has a business. You simply asked if they have seen the new digital business cards. Most people have not, so I hand them my phone they enter their contact info, the digital card is created for me to send to them. Now they are a contact in my phone. I know exactly when they are viewing my card, I get notified. I can also make notes about the prospect, where I met them what they do etc. I can also set up reminder calls to follow up. Most of the time the prospect has no idea what I do till they are viewing my card. I am sharing a tool that can help them with their business, in turn they see what my business is, which can start another conversation. I love these digital business cards because you can have up to 5 videos on your card. So now your products and services become alive. In today's world it's all about technology! Everyone has a phone in their hand 24/7 and will respond to a text five to one over an e-mail.

Communication is one of the keys to success. You must stay in touch with your leaders, your team, your customers and your prospects. If you remain focused on the goal, you will get there!

Be the leader and people will follow you. If you don't have an upline that supports you or helps you, then you MUST become the upline you wished you had. Too many people blame their upline as the reason they have not been successful in network marketing. One of the biggest lessons I learned over the years in network marketing are these eight little words: If it's to be, it's up to me!

Don't listen to the naysayers. Align yourself with positive people. Have a clear vision of what you want and where you are going. I will not allow anyone to steal my dream. I will control my destiny. I will persist until I succeed. Three decades in this industry of network marketing--I guess you could say I have stick-ability.

The biggest thing I have learned about myself in running my business is I love people! I am the happiest when I am around people. I love to meet new people and find out about their lives and what they value in life. Treat people the way you want to be treated.

Every person you meet, look at them as if they had a stamp on their forehead that said, "Make Me Feel Important"! I love that I am in the people business and energy just happens to be my service. 90% of my success depends on my attitude. Therefore, I must always be attending self-improvement seminars as a huge part of my success.

What three resources do you feel anyone in network marketing needs? Why?

#1 Find a mentor and do what they do. Read what they read. You must be coachable and willing to do what they tell you to do. Make sure you pick a mentor who has the success you are looking to achieve. Then commit to the relationship and watch your business soar.

#2 Start building your library of books and CD's about Network Marketing. Become a student of Network Marketing. To become a great leader, you will need to learn about leadership, Communication, Marketing, Mindset and presentation skills. The good news is there are hundreds of books & tapes to learn how to be successful in Network Marketing. Set a goal to read just 30 minutes a day. That would equal 1-2 books a month. Reading 12 to 24 books in a year would make a huge impact not only on your business but your life. "Formal education will make you a living; self-education will make you a fortune." Jim Rohn

#3 Attend live seminars and take online courses outside of your companies corporate events. This may be outside of your comfort zone, but it is a MUST to grow both personally and professionally. Ask any top income earner in Network Marketing and they will tell you they have spent thousands of dollars investing in themselves.

Bring your downline with you to these events. I try to attend 3 to 4 live events a year outside of our annual conventions. These Events will motivate you. Plus, you meet lots of new people and learn new things to share with your team.

How do you keep yourself motivated and encouraged when things don't go right?

When I am in my office, I am surrounded by pictures of my grandkids, motivational quotes, and my vision board. If I start feeling down, I just take a minute and reflect on my why. I will read and reflect on all the goals and dreams I have on my vision board. I look at what I have already accomplished for the year and immediately I will have that attitude of gratitude right back.

My bookshelf in my office is filled with hundreds of books on personal growth and development. I start each day reading and end each day reading. I love music, and upbeat music can snap me right back into my happy place faster than anything. I put on some Bon Jovi "It's my life" and that will usually fire me right back up.

Staying plugged into positive people who lift you up and not drag you down. I have to say I am excellent at taking care of me. I get monthly massages, manicures, pedicures, facials. You must take care of yourself before you can take care of others! I avoid conflict. I detach myself from negative people. Most importantly Read, Read, Read! Readers are leaders and leaders are readers.

What advice would you give to a woman entrepreneur who is ready to take her business to the next level?

1. Talk less, listen more! Find out what the person wants and needs in their life and show them how they can achieve it! God gave you two ears and only one mouth. Hmmm, something to think about.

2. Keep it simple! Never do anything other people can't copy. People need to follow in your footsteps. If you make it complicated, you will lose people along the way.

3. Believe in yourself: Believe more in your dreams more than your doubts. Don't settle for anything but the best that life has to offer.

To me, success is being happy with what you have while you pursue all that you want! I learned from Tom Hopkins almost 25 years ago: "Success is the continuous journey towards the achievement of pre-determined, worthwhile goals." So, I set goals in all areas of my life: health, finance, relationships, personal growth, and in business.

Success is an everyday job. Once you achieve one goal, you must always have the next goal ready to work towards. As long as I am staying consistent and persistent towards achieving my goals, I am successful. Success is measured by how many times one can fail and try again. Never give up or quit, and you will succeed. To me, success is adding value to my company but also to my overall life and the lives of other people.

Believe you can become wealthy! You are worthy of wealth!

Three B's to Success:
1. Believe in yourself
2. Believe in your product
3. Believe in your company

Build great relationships with people. We all do business with people we know, like and trust. Find a mentor and do what they do. Read what they read.

Get the vision of what you are willing to work towards. Make a treasure map or vision board. Search through magazines and clip out what is a goal, a vision, a dream. It might be a cruise, Disneyland with the family, a lake house, a new car, sunset on the beach, a new computer, new furniture, etc. Paste all these items on a poster board and look at them daily.

Work on yourself. Attend more seminars. Give yourself permission to succeed. Take care of yourself first and DREAM big. Just decide to decide to go for greatness and make it happen! Step outside of your comfort zone and take a risk! You will never know until you try.

What are your insights about the direct selling/network marketing industry that will help women starting their own independent consultant business?

Of course, I am very passionate about the direct selling/network marketing industry. This industry allowed me to be a work from home mom when my kids were little. I was 26 years old with a 1, 3 and 5-year-old kids. This industry allowed me to be a full-time mom never missing anything in my kids' lives. Now 30 years later network marketing allows me the time freedom to spend with my eight grandchildren, husband, and kids, living life on our terms!

Here are just a few of the benefits of being involved in this industry:

1. Time Freedom
2. Being Your Own Boss
3. Financial Freedom
4. Personal Development
5. Fun
6. Helping Others
7. Work from Home
8. Making a Difference
9. Debt Freedom
10. Meeting New People

I am a network marketing professional focused on helping people live a life of Abundance! Zig Ziglar said it best! "Help people get what they want, and you will get everything in life you want." The most successful people in network marketing are the ones who build leaders and make them independent leaders of their success line.

What book(s) would you recommend to women starting their own business?

I learned from the great Jim Rohn that there are three things in life to leave behind to your children!

1. Your library of all the great books you have read
2. Your photos

3. Your journals

So here is a list of a few of my favorite books that helped me get started in network marketing.

- *Your First Year in Network Marketing/ Mark Yarnell*
- *Beach Money/ Jordan Adler*
- *The Four-Year Career/ Richard Brooke*
- *The Power of Focus /Jack Canfield Mark, Victor Hansen & Les Hewitt*
- *The Success Principles/ Jack Canfield*
- *MLM Nuts and $ Bolts/* by Jan Ruhe
- *The Compound Effect* /by Darren Hardy
- *Go Pro* /by Eric Worre
- *Being the Best You Can Be in MLM* /by John Kalench
- *Dare to Dream and Work to Win* / by Dr. Tom Barrett
- *Feed the Good Dog: Making the Choice to Succeed /* by Paul McGabe
- *Secrets of the Millionaire Mind/* by T Harv Ekert
- *The Seasons of Life* /by Jim Rohn
- *The Five Major Pieces to the Life Puzzle/* by Jim Rohn
- *Developing the Leader Within You/* by John C Maxwell
- *Developing the Leader Around You* /by John C. Maxwell
- *Awaken the Giant Within/* by Anthony Robbins
- *Don't Sweat the Small Stuff and it's all Small Stuff* /by Richard Carson PhD
- *The Ambitious Woman*/Esther Spina
- *Building Lifetime Loyal Relationships/* Alice Hinckley & Melynda Lilly

Learn more about Melynda Lilly

Melynda began her career in direct sales and network marketing over 29 years ago. She has built large organizations with the goal of helping average people earn an above average income so they can do things in life they are passionate about.

Melynda is incredibly passionate about her family which includes her husband of 37 years, Mark, three grown children and eight beautiful grandchildren.

Connect with Melynda
www.lilly.energygoldrush.com
mlilly@flash.net
www.facebook.com/melyndalilly
www.facebook.com/ambitwithmelynda
www.twitter.com/mklilly
www.linkedin.com/melyndalilly

ALICE HINCKLEY

Tell us a little about yourself.

I am grateful to lead an exceptional life. I've been married to my precious husband, Bob, for over twelve years. My heart overflows with love for him. Bob is my most raving fan. I consider myself abundantly blessed to be his wife. I am affectionately known as his "little redhead." We currently live in Dallas, Texas, with our two sweet four-legged children, Allie and Baxter. We bought a home in Hot Springs Village, Arkansas, about a year ago and are transitioning to semi-retirement this year.

I enjoy playing tennis and golf. I absolutely love to read. Also, traveling to be with friends is a regular past-time. I have the most wonderful goddess girlfriends around the world. We travel to create magic moments together. One of my favorites is the annual trip to Miraval Spa & Resort in Arizona. Healthy food, incredible spa treatments, fun exercise, and challenges. Life is a gift to be treasured. My daily intention is to embrace each moment.

I am a master networker. My family moved a lot during my upbringing, so I learned to adapt and make new friends. I have always had the entrepreneurial bug. As a teenager in New Jersey, I talked my mom into becoming an Avon lady, so we could do the business together. It makes me smile thinking how proud I was to have my first checking account.

My college days were spent at Baylor University in Waco, Texas, earning a bachelor's degree in business administration. After graduating, I moved to Dallas to work as a Certified Public Accountant (CPA). After several years, I realized sitting in a cubicle preparing tax returns day-after-day was going to turn me into a grumpy old woman.

The opportunity to start my own tax practice presented itself, and I jumped in-becoming a full-time entrepreneur. I was finally able to set my own schedule, make my own decisions, and grow a business. Always a nerd at heart, I enjoyed the numbers and putting the pieces of the puzzles together-I just enjoyed it so much more with the freedom to manage my own time.

The only unsettling part of having my own income tax practice was being home alone all day working. I discovered network marketing when I attended a Discovery Toys home party to buy gifts at Christmas. I was so eager to join Discovery Toys and start a business where I had a network of other women to connect with regularly. I earned the annual trips with Discovery Toys to Cancun, Hong Kong, Hawaii, and other exotic locations. I earned a trip during my very first year and then proceeded to earn President's Club level recognition two years in a row. Pretty good for an accountant with no children sharing educational toys with the world. So many great memories and lifetime friendships were built while I was a part of Discovery Toys.

I had become officially hooked on the idea of network marketing. Started making it a point to support any friends and family who started their own businesses. I still do support as many network marketing entrepreneurs as possible. How? If I can buy a product from a network marketing company, I do it. If you look around our house, you will find products from Melaluca, Mary Kay, Isagenix, Stella & Dot, Herbalife…I could go on and on! I challenge you to support network marketing entrepreneurs. You want them to support you, so let's all support one another.

Through my involvement with network marketing, I was introduced to personal development: Constant And Never-Ending Improvement-CANI. Growing and learning new skills became a part of my daily routine back in 1990. I still listen to podcasts, audio books, and CDs on a daily basis. I read books and attend events regularly to improve myself both personally and professionally. As a matter of fact, when I meet new people, I always like to find out what they are reading to improve themselves personally and professionally.

My quest for continued personal growth led me to becoming an independent contractor for the Anthony Robbins Companies. It was such an incredible experience! For about seven years, I had the privilege of traveling all over the world supporting Tony as the Main Room Manager at live events. I am blessed to have visited many cities throughout the United States, as well as Europe, Australia, Singapore, and Fiji. I learned so much from Tony Robbins on financial mastery, relationship mastery, health and wellness, business strategies, and so much more. I was introduced to world-renowned speakers and experts such as Erin Brockovich, Gen. Norman Schwarzkopf, Brian Tracy, Deepak Chopra, Captain Gerald Coffee, and many more thought leaders and teachers. One of my all-time favorites is Kathy Buckley. She is a deaf comedian. A true inspiration. You can find her on YouTube. Laughter is so good for you! Kathy will teach you life lessons while making you laugh hysterically.

When I wasn't traveling with the Robbins Team, I embraced a part-time commission sales position in the mortgage industry. Mortgages were new to me. The perfect thing for a nerdy accountant who liked numbers but also wanted to interact with people. My years in the mortgage business revealed my deep desire to educate others. Buying a house is one of the largest investments most people ever make. Helping my clients understand the process while being a calm, compassionate presence for them made me passionate about building the business.

The mortgage industry slowed down drastically around the time Bob and I were introduced to Ambit Energy. We are celebrating our tenth anniversary with Ambit Energy this year. We are so proud of the hundreds of people on our team. We are passionate about helping them design their lives by achieving financial freedom. Speaking and training for Ambit Energy reinforced my desire to help others grow in their skills. For several years now, I have traveled within the United States teaching finance, business writing, group communication, networking, rapport building, and leadership skills.

Share with us why you wanted to start this business and how you went about it.

I have been a network marketing professional with Ambit Energy for almost ten years. I help people save money on electricity and natural gas. Many even earn the right to free energy month after month. More importantly, I teach others to build a business where they leverage the efforts of an entire team. Each month, my business partners get paid a portion of every electricity and natural gas customer won by their team. When the customers pay their monthly utility bills, we each earn a residual income. The fifteenth of every month is always a day for celebration in the Hinckley household when we see the fruits of our labor deposited into our bank account even before we are out of bed.

We worked diligently during the first few years to build a strong foundation for our Ambit Energy business. I'm excited to share that when we bought our new home in Arkansas, we paid for it in **cash**! The money we earned from our Ambit business enabled us to be debt free!

My tenure in network marketing led me to create another business teaching entrepreneurs the skills they need to succeed. I now speak to teams in all types of network marketing companies. I have created online courses to complement my books. Learn more at http://www.yourlightbulbmoments.com/products/ I even have my own TV show on the Direct Sales TV Network (Apple & Roku), Lightbulb Moments with Alice Hinckley. View my shows at http://directsales.tv/channel/lightbulb-moments/ My passion is helping entrepreneurs, especially women in network marketing, make more money and keep more of the money they make. Money creates freedom and allows you to design the life of your dreams.

What was the biggest obstacle you've encountered? How did you overcome it?

The biggest obstacle in network marketing is making sure you are working with people who truly desire success. They must realize success requires an investment of time and effort. Because most network marketing companies do not require a huge investment of money to get started, sometimes people do not take it seriously. They choose to quit at the first sign of rejection or with their first small failure because they don't have that much money in the game.

Three practices have been implemented to help people stay engaged. The first is to understand why the new team member wants to succeed. Help them define success. It is different for everyone. Some people want to make $500 a month to pay for their children's extra-curricular activities, while others want to replace their entire family income. Once you know their definition of success for their new business, you can work with them to set up a strategy of time invested each week, number of contacts made, etc.

The second practice is to set the expectation early on that disappointment is inevitable. Ambit Energy allows families to save money on their electricity and natural gas bills. Many of our team members and customers have earned free electricity-yes, their energy bill is free every month! When new people join our team, they obviously see the value, and most cannot understand why everyone would not want to have their utility service with Ambit Energy. With any network marketing company, the new team member is joining because they see value in the product or service the company has to offer.

The hard truth is at the beginning of building their business, someone who they thought would support them unconditionally-a family member or close friend-is going to say no and will not become a customer. Many reasons exist for this rejection. Sometimes, people are afraid that you'll change and leave them behind. Other times, people think you won't stay with the company.

Even still, there are people who are just afraid of change. The bottom line is to make sure new team members are aware how often friends and family are more negative than positive at the beginning of their journey. The positive side of this situation comes after the new team member starts having some success; many of the "no" responses they received will turn into a "yes."

The third practice is to make sure new team members start earning money immediately. Ambit Energy has excellent bonus payouts for new people gathering customers during their first month. Most network marketing companies have some sort of "fast-start bonus" to encourage new team members at the beginning. Nothing teaches a new team member network marketing is going to create a new stream of income for their family like when they begin receiving checks. Therefore, the goal is to help the new team member experience success by teaching them how to gather customers and reinforcing their success by recognizing them publicly. By nature, humans like to be appreciated and complimented. Therefore, make sure to not only personally congratulate a new team member for early achievements, but be sure to tell other team members about the new person's success as well.

What have been your best practices to grow, nurture, and retain your client/customer base?

It is all about staying connected. Yes, you can send out your company newsletter or updates, but you must also have a personal connection with your customers. You want to be connected on social media. Create private groups for your customers, and share valuable information in the group. You won't always be selling. You might be offering recipes or fashion advice or just plain old encouragement.

Personally, I believe in the lost art of sending handwritten 'thank you' notes. People really appreciate the effort made when they receive one. It helps connect them to you. For years, I have had magnets with the company website and phone numbers on them. I send the magnets with the 'thank you' notes, so now, my business card is on the refrigerator. The idea is for them to think of you whenever they have a need for a product you offer.

Also, remember to send personalized instant messages or texts to check on customers a week or so after they sign on. It only takes a couple of minutes to continue to solidify your relationship for the long-term.

What have been your best practices to grow, nurture, and retain your team?

Once again, connection is the key! When new team members join, we make a phone call and send an email or text to introduce ourselves. We want them to know they have a support system. We have been in network marketing for years. We can help them build a strong team and a lucrative income without making some of the mistakes we did along the way.

We also make "elevator calls." In other words, we will call a couple of people each day just to encourage them in their business and life. We lift them up with our words, which is why it's called an "elevator call." We ask if they have questions or need any assistance.

Often times, we end up leaving messages. Great! They now have a recording of someone who believes in them.

Recognition is so vital to nurturing a team. People want to be congratulated for a job well done. Recognize them in front of their peers. We applaud people for attending events, earning their Fast Start Bonuses, rank advancement, and customer gathering-all key elements of building a long-term residual income.

Hold team events. You can have a picnic or potluck. People bond when they get to know one another. Team members realize they are a part of something bigger than themselves. Do you have a team spread out across the US or the world? Host a video conferencing party! Have everyone join the video at a certain time. Spend an hour getting to know the new people. Choose who will share by asking who has a birthday in June or March or November. Let those people share why they joined the team. Be sure to include some recognition in all team events.

Be careful at any event. Don't let the negative people take over. Set the stage in advance for no complaining. You can take questions, of course. Just remember it is your team and you are the leader. If someone starts to complain or be negative, stop them and set up a time to discuss the issue with them one-on-one.

What have been the most successful marketing strategies you have used to grow your business?

Referrals. Once you have a satisfied customer, they are free advertising for you. Ask them who else in their life would benefit from your product. Remember those 'thank you' notes I like to send? I always ask for referrals in them.

Many companies allow customers to receive free products or services when they host an event and bring their friends. It can be in person or online. What a great way to meet your customer's circle of influence! When they host for you, they are endorsing you. Thank them, and then take exceptional care of all their friends since they referred you and your product to them.

Another strategy is to ask your most active customers to join your team. When someone starts sending me lots of referrals or using more of my products, I always make sure to let them know they could make an income by joining my team. You must ASK them to join your team. Do not assume they know they can, or that you would be thrilled to have them on your team. ASK them to join your team!

What three resources do you feel anyone in network marketing needs? Why?

First is to create a personal board of directors. Invite three to six individuals that you meet with on a quarterly basis in a group or one-on-one. Consider who you ask to be on your board based on your personal and professional goals. If you want to improve your prospecting, find someone who always seems to have plenty of potential customers and team members to meet. Let the person know you admire them and ask them to support you with insights. If you meet with your board as a group, set a time limit of 90 minutes. Everyone's time is valuable. If you meet individually, half an hour is sufficient. Be prepared with questions. Be respectful.

Second is to have an accountability partner. Find someone who is successful in their network marketing company. It doesn't have to be in your own company. Make sure it isn't one of your closest friends. They will let you off the hook too often. Set up a time to have a phone call with them on a weekly basis. Share your goals for your business for that week. Ask the question: What has to happen for this week to be a success for you? For years, I had a Monday morning call with a dear friend who had long tenure in another company. We shared ideas, encouragement, and our weekly goals. When you know someone is expecting you to take action, it propels you forward.

Last, but certainly not least, you must have a follow-up system. Because we are all out and about networking, I like to use Shuffle digital business cards, which include a follow-up system. On the spot, I enter a new person's name, cell number, and email in my phone. Right then, I text them my digital card with all my contact information, social media, and even links to my website. Learn more about this inexpensive and highly effective tool at www.elify.com/alice.hinckley People will be amazed at how high-tech you are, and you will benefit from the follow-up reminders you set.

How do you keep yourself motivated and encouraged when things don't go right?

Let's consider four ideas to help you stay focused on a positive mindset in your business:

First, a good friend and mentor taught me to discipline my disappointments. Yes, you are going to have challenges. You are going to fail. You are going to make bad decisions. People are going to hurt you or disappoint you. Go ahead and feel hurt, sad, angry, frustrated, etc. Then **move on**! If you choose to spend hours (or days!) in your negative reaction, you are stealing time from productive activities.

The questions I now choose to ask myself after I have a brief pity party are: What have I learned from this situation? How should I act in the future to avoid a similar negative result? What is positive about this situation?

I always remind myself that "success is not permanent." Failure is not fatal. It is the courage to go on that truly matters.

Second, I do not to compare myself to others, or judge myself. Network marketing allows everyone to move at their own pace. I have always had an achiever personality. When I joined my current company, I also had other businesses, and still do. In the past, I would compare my extremely part-time efforts and results to those of the people who were working forty to sixty hours a week. I was pretty hard on myself for the first few years, because others were building faster and had larger teams and incomes. However, I finally realized my part-time efforts were consistent and producing strong results to last a lifetime. Now, I choose to compare my results with my efforts and not worry about the results others are achieving- except to congratulate them.

Third, always remember there is a difference between easy and simple. Ambit Energy and network marketing are simple businesses, but there is nothing easy about them. You have to be consistent in your prospecting, in supporting your team, and in attending events.

When people say, "This is easy, anybody can do it," I disagree with them. It is simple and makes sense on a very basic level. However, it is not easy. It is work. That is why it is called net**work** marketing. You have to put in the effort to get the results. You have to put your efforts in the right area and with the right people. Early on, I gave everyone who joined the team the same amount of time and effort. Now, I know to crawl with those who are crawling, walk with those who are walking, and run with those who are running.

Fourth, some people do not want your help. Even though my network marketing company has a proven system, and people are making hundreds, thousands, and even hundreds of thousands of dollars a month, there will be new team members who choose not to plug into the system because they believe there is a better way. Usually, this involves a short cut they believe will produce results more quickly than anyone else. I have finally learned to offer my help to these people by continually inviting them to meetings, training events, and conference calls. It is their business. I must release them to learn on their own that the system works and there is no reason to reinvent the process.

What advice would you give to a woman entrepreneur who is ready to take her business to the next level?

Do not take advice from someone who does not have what you want. It always amuses me when people offer advice to others when they don't have the results in their lives the person they are talking to wants. Find someone who has accomplished what you want to, and follow in their footsteps. Women like helping each other. Having a role model or mentor who has achieved what you want to will help you avoid the mistakes they made. Mentors advise you on what worked for them and what was a catastrophe. When you ask someone to mentor you, follow what they advise. If not, you are wasting their time and yours. It's like having a recipe-follow it, and you'll get a fabulous dish. Skip one or two steps, and you'll end up with a complete mess.

What are your insights about the direct selling/network marketing industry that will help women who are growing their own independent consultant business?

Three vital insights for building a successful network marketing business:

First, always be prospecting! Become a Master Networker. Every time you leave your house, you are networking. Make it a goal to meet one new person a day. Have a plan. This doesn't mean to go out and tell everyone about your business. Prospecting and networking is about building relationships. Smile. Say hello. If you are at your nephew's soccer game, talk to the other spectators. Find out about them. Ask lots of questions. As Stephen R. Covey taught us, "Be more interested than interesting."

Second, personal development is crucial to success. You must always be honing your skills and your character. Read. Listen to audio books and podcasts. Attend events from your company or personal development experts. Watch TED Talks. Some of my personal favorite mentors are Jim Rohn, Wayne Dyer, Jack Canfield, John Maxwell, Denise Duffield-Thomas, Don Miguel Ruiz, Joel Osteen, Andy Andrews, Mark Batterson-I could go on and on.

Find an area you want to improve on and ask other successful people who they enjoy learning from in that area. Two of my favorite questions to ask successful businesspeople I meet are, "What is your favorite business or personal development book?" and "What are you reading now?" You will get some great insights. Recently, I asked these questions of a woman I admire, and she shared some resources for having an exceptionally fulfilling marriage. Just like you work on your business relationships, keeping your personal relationships engaged and empowering is vital for living an extraordinary life.

Last, remember to define success for yourself. Success is about freedom. Freedom to choose what you do with your time. Freedom to do the things that are important to you. I measure success by whether someone else has control of when you can or cannot do things. Another measure of success is being able to meet a need when you see it because you have the financial means. Success is having the funds available to do things like attend a friend's destination wedding without stressing about your finances. When a friend invites you to the beach for a week to celebrate her husband's sixtieth birthday, do you just have to check your schedule for other commitments, or do you have to ask permission from someone to be able to go? Do you have the financial resources to obtain airline tickets and enjoy great meals while at the beach?

Success is not necessarily being a multi-millionaire. Success is having the choice to enrich your life at any moment with both time and financial freedom. What is your "Financial Freedom Number?" How much money do you need every month to cover all of your expenses and not have to work? You can include the basics such as food, shelter, and transportation, but you must also include entertainment, travel, donating to charity-whatever is important to you to live the lifestyle you have always dreamed of. For me, this embodies true success.

What book(s) would you recommend to women who are starting their own businesses?

Because I am an avid reader, this list could be pages long. Here are a few of my favorites:
- *The Noticer* by Andy Andrews
- *The Richest Man in Babylon* by George Clason
- *The Go-Giver Series* by Bob Burg & John David Mann
- *Go Pro* by Eric Worre
- *The Happiness Advantage* by Shawn Achor
- *Lead the Field* by Earl Nightingale
- *The Four-Year Career for Women* by Kimmy Brooke
- *You are a Badass with Money* by Jen Sincero
- *How to Make People Like You in 90 Seconds* by Nicholas Boothman
- *The Tipping Point* by Malcolm Gladwell
- *The Ambitious Woman* by Esther Spina
- *Becoming a Person of Influence* by John Maxwell

Of course, my own books have been a help to so many:

- *Building Lifetime Relationships* by Melynda Lilly & Alice Hinckley
- *Nail it in 90! For Direct Sales & Network Marketing* by Kim Johnson & Alice Hinckley
- *Think Like a CEO* by Alice Hinckley with Elizabeth McCormick
- *Behind Her Brand: Women of Influence* by Alice Hinckley & others

- *Behind Her Brand: Entrepreneur Edition Volume 4* by Alice Hinckley & others
- *Women Entrepreneur Extraordinaire* by Alice Hinckley & others

All my books can be found on my author page at Amazon.com

Learn more about Alice Hinckley

Alice Hinckley is a network marketing professional, dynamic trainer and admired mentor for entrepreneurs especially women building a business in direct sales or network marketing. With over twenty-five years' experience as an entrepreneur, Alice recognizes one small change or step can produce far-reaching results. She is passionate about empowering people to excel in all areas of life. Over the past decade, Alice has gained particular popularity with women in the network marketing and direct sales industry by helping them create steady income from a home-based business.

Alice brings extensive experience to her presentations with a background in personal development, mortgage & real estate, network marketing & direct selling, accounting & income tax, coaching & speaking, event production, business development, and mentoring & training. Alice has achieved the coveted President's Club in both corporate America and network marketing. She has traveled the globe with inspirational speakers while maintaining her own accounting practice.

As a top-rated speaker and mentor, Alice's engaging style coupled with her experience captures audiences of one to one thousand. Her goal is to strategically prepare her audience with simple tools they can implement immediately to begin improving the results in their business.

Alice has a reputation for an insightful, pragmatic approach to business and life. She has shared her experience and wisdom in many ways including co-authoring six books and speaking for groups and conferences all over the United States.

On a more personal note, Alice is a Southern girl at heart. Currently residing in Dallas, Texas, with my incredible husband, Bob, and our fur babies, Allie and Baxter. Alice & Bob have purchased their retirement home and are transitioning to living in Arkansas. Alice plays tennis & golf, reads, travels, entertain friends, experience personal development and basically enjoy life!

One of the greatest blessings in my life is my husband, Bob. He is smart, fun, loving, compassionate and so much more. God truly shined a light into my life when we met. Am grateful for our fourteen plus years together. Looking forward to decades more.

One thing I know for sure, my life is magnificent because I intentionally design my life. Do all my plans work out perfectly? Heck no! However, the journey is absolutely amazing! I wake up each day excited for the people I can serve and the experiences of the day. Looking forward to each day and continuing to create a life overflowing with love and happiness.

Connect with Alice:

www.YourLightbulbMoments.com

alice@yourlightbulbmoments.com

www.facebook.com/lightbulbmoments/

www.facebook.com/alice.hinckley

www.instagram.com/alicehinckley

Via Alice's Digital Business Card: http://bit.ly/AHDigitalCard

AMY JIMENEZ

Tell us a little about yourself.

My name is Amy Jimenez, and I have been married to my husband Kevin for twenty-one years. For the past nineteen years, we have resided in Charleston, SC. We have two beautiful and amazingly witty children, a 16-year-old daughter and a 12-year-old son. My faith and my family have always been the two cornerstones of my life, and I have genuinely cherished every milestone with my children. My faith was called to action in 2006 when I received the life-altering news that I had Multiple Sclerosis. I had just given birth to our second child and noticed something wasn't quite right. My balance was off, I couldn't see out of my right eye when my body temperature increased, and I was falling a lot. I am a klutz anyway, but I was falling much more than usual. I've always said that people have two choices in life when you are faced with life-changing news: you can retreat, or you can fight. You can choose despair, or you can choose joy. It was my turn to see how I would take my own advice.

Share with us how you got started in your business and why you wanted to start this business.

A few years ago, I had a friend approach me about an idea he had. He is a physician and had spent a few years researching an emerging trend in science and beauty and asked me to be a part of it. You know when you hear an idea, and you can't stop thinking about it? When this idea consumes your every thought? That is what this "idea" did to me. I couldn't sleep because I had so many thoughts and visions running through my head. I kept a journal beside my bed so I wouldn't forget anything. I would dream something, wake up, and jot it in my notebook. I think, for me, building this business gave me something to dream about again.

Life can be so difficult. You see so much pain and hear so many stories that break your heart. To have something to dream about is so important. We all have plans for our future, but how many of us have had our dreams happen as we thought? One of my favorite quotes is "God laughs while we plan." Our Creator has a path for us, and most of the time it looks a lot different than what we envision. I would never have asked for MS, but what it has given me is a sincere appreciation for every moment. I can still see my kids playing sports-thank God for my sight. I can still walk around although I have a limp-thank God for my legs! I can still talk and laugh-thank God for my voice! I can still breathe-thank God for my lungs! Hope is essential, even in the darkest times! Find your dream again. Do not let the darkness of this fallen world extinguish your light.

What was the biggest obstacle you've encountered? How did you overcome it?

When you are building a business from the ground level, there are so many challenges. It's like having 100 ingredients in front of you without a recipe. You have an idea on how to put it all together based on personal experiences, learning from others, research, and trial and error, but will it work? Have you combined the right amount of everything to make your creation a success? You don't know until you hit the start button.

The other thing I have learned is you cannot make everyone happy! I tend to be a people pleaser, and I truly desire the best for everyone. Sometimes, this backfires on me, because I focus on the wrong issues, the wrong people, and the wrong causes. I expend so much energy fixing everything that I lose sight of what is working and the people that are making the right things happen! The older I get, the more I realize that some people will never change. You can try to make them happy and content, but they must find this within themselves. I have learned that I am not responsible for others' bad choices and negativity. As long as I know I have done everything in my power to help them succeed, I can rest easy. Lead by example and let people know from the start you are there to help them every step of the way. If they drain you emotionally, then know when to step back.

What have been your best practices to grow, nurture, and retain your client/customer base?

The best way to grow your business is to follow-up. I cannot stress this enough. You must regularly check in with your existing customers and your team daily. One of my mentors taught me to send a hand-written thank you note after every sale or appointment you get. This is a lost art. People want to feel valued and appreciated for their time and money spent with you. I always recommend that the first day you start your business, get stationery made with your company's logo. I carry mine with me wherever I go, and as soon as my appointment is over, I write the note and drop it in the mail. If you wait, you will forget!

What have been your best practices to grow, nurture, and retain your team?

It's so important to check in with your team DAILY. As your organization grows, this job will become more difficult, but you need to check the pulse of your team daily. Let them know they are valued and appreciated and listen to what's going on with their business and their lives. I always start my calls with a five minute check-in on how they are doing personally! Make sure they know that you care about their successes and struggles. This business we are in is all about people and relationships. It's very easy to get caught up in the "churn and burn" mentality of our industry, but you must relate to your customers and your team on a personal level. Know their husbands' and children's names, know what they love to do in their free time, find out their favorite restaurants and places to travel. The more you pour into your team, the more success you will have. Make sure you run your business like a "family" business, where you have each other's backs at all times!

I was also taught that it's a lot easier to nurture the team you already have than neglecting your current reps while trying to find new ones. As you have learned, finding people to sell your product isn't an easy task. Think about the time it takes to bring people into your business...the countless hours spent on training and nurturing. You must do everything you can to make sure your "family" feels valued and loved. Get them to a level where they are confident enough to sell on their own but still know you are there for them when they need you...that they never were just a number. A critical rule while nurturing, however, is learning when to call it quits if someone is draining you of time and energy. If the only conversations you have with them are rooted in negativity and complaining, then this business might not be a good fit for them. The more I am in this space, the more I have learned that I want to surround myself with people that share the same goals, values, and vision as me. If they do not share your same belief system, then they probably won't be a good fit for your team. I have learned this the hard way more times than not. Close the door if the door needs to be closed, I promise you and the rest of your existing team will benefit from it. Nothing poisons an organization more than someone who carries negative energy, nothing you do will make them happy or content. I can promise you that!

What have been the most successful marketing strategies you have used to grow your business?

The best marketing strategy to grow my business is, never be afraid to ask for referrals. If you have a fantastic product that people love, they will WANT to tell their friends. Even if they have no interest in selling it, they will want other people they know and love to benefit from it as well. I think this is one of the hardest things to train ourselves to do. But, it's the quickest way to generate 5-10 leads that you would have never secured without asking. But you must time it correctly. You cannot, on your first meeting, ask for the referral. Make sure you have raving fans of your product and raving fans of you. This skill will take a little time to cultivate, but I have always said that people love to help. The best thing about referrals is that they are free! All you have to do is ask. I would also be willing to offer your customers an incentive to refer their friends. Such incentives could include a free product, a gift card to their favorite restaurant or coffee shop, or even an afternoon playdate with your children so they can run some errands, without having to hire a babysitter. Get creative with your referral gifts to let your customers know just how much their referral means to you and your growing franchise.

What three resources do you feel anyone in network marketing needs? Why?

The three resources that are essential in maintaining and growing your network marketing business are the right marketing pieces, proper tools to help you follow up with your customers and your organization and a reliable way to track your business' growth, decline, sales and personal goals you have set for your franchise. Marketing pieces: Make sure you have the proper tools to spread the word about your business. Use the resources your company has designed for you to your advantage. Most companies are trending towards "cloud" based technology, allowing you to download and print items directly from home. With today's digital age, I prefer having a file of documents that I can email or text quickly to a potential customer or client. Make sure you keep your initial touch point short and sweet. For example, a quick 2-minute video or fact sheet about your product is a great follow up to a first conversation. If someone is interested in being a customer, make sure you send them information on what you are selling only. Don't send them anything on the business side until you know they love your product. You don't want to overwhelm them with information!

Follow up tools and tracking: If your company doesn't provide you with this in your back office, I suggest creating a spreadsheet to help you follow up with your team and customers. Design an Excel spreadsheet that includes the person's name, address, email, cell phone, date of purchase, and what they purchased. Make sure you include columns that track when your first follow up should occur.

When building my business, I used the following system to stay connected with my customers. REMEMBER, FOLLOW UP IS CRUCIAL IN MAINTAINING AND GROWING YOUR BUSINESS!

1. First touch point: Remember to send your handwritten thank you note. Carry them with you and write it immediately. Have a mini post office set up in your car with your notes, stamps, business cards and a pen, so you don't have to wait until you get home.

2. Second touch point: Once you know they have received their product or service, text to make sure they received everything they ordered, thank them again, and see if they have any questions.

3. Third touch point: seven to ten days after touch point two, gauge how well they like your product and see if they have any concerns or questions. You never want your customer to feel as if they were "just a quick sale." Let them know how much they are valued and appreciated!

4. Fourth touch point: Around day 30, follow up with a phone call to make sure they love your product. This is the perfect time to ask for any referrals. If they have become a fan and love the customer experience you have provided for them, they will refer their friends!

Finally, learn and use your back office as a business tool. The majority of network marketing companies have fantastic software that provides you with a digital pulse on the state of your franchise. It can track new customers, reorders, your organization's trends, and your revenue. Make sure you check this often. I always laugh that if my company could see how many times a day I check my organization's sales, they would think I'm slightly neurotic! If you notice a particular zip code that is growing in your organization, find out what they are doing differently! Follow the trends in your organization closely and use these tools to your advantage. If you don't know how to use your back-office, ask someone that is tech-savvy in your company for help!

How do you keep yourself motivated and encouraged when things don't go right?

The most important thing to remember daily is the ONE thing that made you fall in love with your product and company, right from the start! We can become so beat down by hearing "no" so many times that we start to believe that what we are selling isn't as wonderful as we once thought it was. The reality of it all is that you will become unmotivated and discouraged almost daily, and that's ok! Sales aren't easy, and you must grow thick skin very quickly! People can pick up on and feed off your excitement, or lack thereof when you are talking about your product.

Think about it this way, when you are shopping, who do you like to buy from? The sales clerk that compliments you, acts happy and enthusiastic, gets excited and shares that excitement or the one that is hunched over in the corner, barely smiling, and ultimately beat down from the morning rush? Smiles sell! A few weeks ago, we were at a bustling amusement park, and I said to our children, "look around and search for the people who are smiling and laughing; the ones that are having a good time!" Honestly, there weren't many to be found! These people were on vacation for goodness sakes, and most of the passersby looked miserable! I would say 98/100 people were continually frowning, walked with a negative posture, and were yelling at either their spouses or their children. I pointed out to my 16-year-old how attractive smiling is. To see someone, with a smile on their face, allows you to feel comfortable and relaxed. Find the joy and gratitude in everything, everyone, and every situation!

Also, you must always stay hungry for the next sale and when you have that win, make sure you celebrate! Let your family know when you had a good day and when you experience success. In one of my previous jobs, the company would force rank you every night based on what you sold. This was so motivating! When I had a good day, I would announce it to my kids, and they would celebrate right alongside me. When I had a bad day, they would tell me not to let anyone beat me, to not give up and to keep selling. Nightly, we had a running joke about one guy that I went head to head within sales. My son, who was six at the time, would shake his head and say the reps name again and again while punching the palm of his hand and shaking his head. We would all laugh, but this motivated me! It kept me hungry, and it allowed my kids to be a part of what I was doing and to learn about achieving goals. Know that things will not go your way most of the time but do not wear your disappointment, move to the next opportunity, and make sure you take the time to celebrate your victories with your loved ones! It makes your job a lot more fun, especially when you are experiencing success!

What advice would you give to a woman entrepreneur who is ready to take her business to the next level?

Make sure you always ask people that have been successful for guidance. These women are successful for a reason. The beauty of asking for advice is that it prevents you from having to re-invent the wheel. If something worked for them, then do it! If something didn't work, then I beg of you to not repeat their mistakes!

Another piece of advice I would offer is to allow yourself to fail. Set super high goals for yourself on what you want for yourself and your family. Where do you see yourself in a year, in five years, and even when you retire? Tell people what you are planning and ask people for help. As I said, people love to help! Send letters to people, tell strangers your dreams, let your family know what you have planned and have them hold you accountable. Then, start preparing to grow your business. Attend local meetings and network with the people there. Once you master this, attend national meetings with other women entrepreneurs. Tell them your dreams and listen to theirs. Do not allow yourself ever to quit. My MS prevents me from doing many things I used to enjoy...walks with my husband, jogs on the beach, spin classes but I can promise you I refuse to give up. We have been gifted this ONE, very BRIEF life, and there is no way I am going to waste it by complaining about everything I can't do. I have found new things that I enjoy, and I will make sure that I am successful at what I can do! If you fail, guess what you tried! This is the gift, knowing that you had a plan, implemented your plan and did everything possible to make it work. No one can take this away from you, win or lose!

What are your insights about the direct selling/network marketing industry that will help women growing their own independent consultant business?

I recommend staying up to date with the emerging trends within network marketing and follow people online that research our industry. It's also super important to also attend every local meeting and training on your product and company conference call to sharpen your skills and knowledge of your company. I know we can all get busy with life, but if you do not stay plugged into your company, your interest and expertise will slowly fade away, until you feel discouraged and want to quit. I would also recommend attending the larger network marketing conferences and your company's conventions. The things you learn and the connections you make at these meetings are invaluable. You will leave motivated, refreshed, and ready to take your business to the next level! These events allow you to be surrounded with women and men that are in the same industry as you! Most of us feel like we are on a deserted island, and no one can understand what we are trying to do when growing our business. People at these meetings are just like you! They understand this space, know that it's not easy and they will encourage you to become better.

What book(s) would you recommend to women starting their own business?

A few of my favorite books that specifically deal with Network Marketing are *Tools of Titans* by Tim Ferriss and *Go Pro* by Eric Worre. I also love any books written by Malcolm Gladwell especially *The Tipping Point, Outliers* and *David and Goliath*. I would also recommend, continually listening to motivational talks on YouTube and I am obsessed with TED Talks! Make sure your mind always plugs into encouraging, motivational books, podcasts, and videos!

Learn more about Amy Jimenez

Amy graduated with a degree in Broadcast Journalism and Communication Studies from Marshall University. Her passion for the media and television allowed her to pursue her dream of on-air production and reporting for television affiliates such as NBC, CBS, and QVC.

She was introduced to network marketing over 30 years ago, by her mom who successfully started and grew her own at home business. Amy loved seeing her mom Alice, interact with her customers and her team and quickly realized this sales model allowed her mom freedom, flexibility, and the potential to earn a substantial income

While working as a broadcast journalist, she was introduced to the world of healthcare and pharmaceuticals and began her career in product development and product sales for many Fortune 500 companies, specializing in women's health and cardiovascular disease.

As her career progressed, she discovered world of genetics and became fascinated with researching disease states associated with genetically based diseases. Her passion lies with people and hearing their stories of what makes them uniquely them. Amy is one of the founders and the current Director of Sales for a DTC genetic based skin care and wellness company.

DAWN FERRENTINO

Tell us a little about yourself.

I am a mom of two boys, Vinnie and Rocco, and a wife of twenty-five years to my husband, Mike. I grew up a middle child, and yes, I had the "middle child syndrome." My parents divorced when I was thirteen, so I lived most of my childhood with my mom and siblings. My sister, Chris, is two years older, and my brother, Mark, was four years younger. I lost my brother to a horrible car accident in 2008 at the young age of thirty-six. My sister and me are best friends, and she recently has become one of my business partners.

I went to college to become an accountant. I loved numbers, but I was extremely shy, so I figured I would be safe in accounting. You don't have to talk to anybody, right? I worked in public at the start of my career, but working in the public sector didn't give me a lot of free time, and I knew I wanted to start a family, so I turned to the private sector.

I had my final job in accounting working for a non-profit company to try to make more time for my family. I also worked a part-time job a few nights a week to make up for the cut in pay when I moved into the non-profit industry. I worked over sixty hours a week between both jobs when I started my network marketing business.

I left my accounting career in March of 2014 to pursue my network business. I am also a business coach, speaker, and trainer. I am certified in Pilates, and I have a passion for health, wellness, and fitness. I have a home on the water on the Jersey shore, and I love the beach, fishing, boating, and pretty much anything to do with the outdoors. I have a chiweenie (part chihuahua and part dachshund) dog named Harley. I love reading and spending time with family and friends around the pool and on the deck watching the sunset.

Share with us how you got started in your business and why you wanted to start this business.

I got started in my business in 2012, when I became a product user of the company I am with. You see, I was looking to make a change physically. I wanted to drop some weight and gain some energy. A friend of mine was sharing about these great products everyone from high school was using to drop weight. I was like, "Hello! I want in…" Well, not right away, but I sat on the sideline and watched. Then one day, I said, "I'm in!" But *only* as a product user. I began using the products. I felt great and decided it was time to share with my friends and family.

I learned what was involved because I figured if I could get my products for free, I'd be in the Eat for Free Club! Who wouldn't want to eat for free? I really didn't want to "start" the business. I really just wanted to get my products paid for. One thing led to another; I kept sharing, and before I knew it, I was all in! I was starting to make some money; my products were paid for quickly, and I knew I had found a solution-not just physically, but also financially.

I grew my business to six figures in nine short months by working hard and getting into action. I was still working my two jobs and trying to manage it all. I built my business in fifteen-minute intervals: lunch breaks, driving to work, driving home from work. I'd get up an hour early or stay up an hour late because I was using NET time (no extra time). When someone tells me they don't have time, I ask them to show me their planner. We *all* have time. It's what we *do* with our time and how important something is we are reaching for. I realized the tv doesn't pay me, so I stopped watching it. The radio always had advertisements, so I started using my car as a rolling university. I used every free minute I could find, and I got into action.

What was the biggest obstacle you've encountered? How did you overcome it?

The biggest obstacle I encountered was wanting everyone I knew to join me. Like, seriously, who wouldn't want to feel good *and* make some money? Well, not that many. I dragged people along at the beginning. I didn't know how to meet people where they were at, and I had attachments to everyone I talked to. I took it all personally! I made it all about me instead of about them.

It took a lot of practice to overcome this. Practice on working on myself. Mindset development. I hired coaches. I listened to podcasts. I began listening to people more. I learned to get to know someone's pain. Match their energy. And if they were not interested in learning how to make money, I took their referrals unapostolically. I stopped building out of desperation in wanting this so much for others and started building out of inspiration.

What have been your best practices to grow, nurture, and retain your client/customer base?

Connecting is one of the things I do best. I created a download called the *Art of Connecting* that my coaching clients receive (also available on my website). The key to success in growing your customer base is consistency and connecting. Network marketing has the word 'work' in it. You have to be in action. You have talk to people. You have to get uncomfortable. I made a commitment to attend a certain amount of network meetings and events weekly. I made a commitment to ask for referrals. I made a commitment to listen (that's why we have two ears), and then share what I have with anyone who will listen in return when I have a solution for them. I have been able to gain customers from my flight heading out to a company convention, or from the lady sitting at the table next to me, because she spoke loud enough for me to hear that she was trying to lose weight. Listen, if someone is talking loud enough in public for me to hear, I do not believe I am eavesdropping.

To retain a customer base, it is all about remembering your customers. Giving them love. Letting them know you care. Contacting them. Texting them. Sending a card in the mail. You don't have a customer the first time they place an order. You have an order. The second time they order, you have a customer. We all know the phrase: "People will not remember what you said to them, but they will remember how you made them feel." Sometimes just a simple text saying, "Congratulations!! You're doing great!" or a hand-written card after they complete their program saying, "Great Job" means so much. You can't succeed in network marketing to the fullest extent without retention. Retention is the bloodline to your business. Keeping your customers happy, educated, inspired, and loved will help immensely with retention.

What have been your best practices to grow, nurture, and retain your team?

Your team becomes like your family. To help your team grow, you love all over them! But you also meet them where they're at. One of the things I do from the very beginning is go down a new member checklist asking a series of questions to help me better understand what they are looking for in this business and setting up their income goals. I want to know right away what kind of income is going to change the quality of their lives right now and why? I want them to feel it. Painting the picture is huge! Even if their goal is creating an additional $500 a month, that picture needs to be painted: What will you pay off? What will this do for you? How will it make you feel? The first level of leadership in my company requires only two customers for my new distributor. We work on reaching that first level of leadership in the first week, if not the first day. My role as their leader is to get them paid. I work very closely with my new people. I stay pretty much hooked at the hip. I use the analogy that I am hooking them on to my belt loop, and when they start to slow down or fall, I'm going to keep pulling them back up. That is our role: to believe in them until they believe in themselves, and then believe in them even more!!

We have weekly team calls. Motivational and inspirational, but also leadership training. Practices, tips, systems, etc. I believe so much in recognition. When someone reaches "consultant" in my organization, no matter how deep they are, they receive a written card congratulating them from me in the mail. If I personally sponsored that person, they will receive a CD. The next level, they receive a book, and the level after that, they receive two books and so forth with the rewards continuing to grow as well.

Retention is important for product users, but it is just as important for your team. I involve my team in many of the decisions I make. I have the team lead calls. I have the team train at events. That's one way to keep the team feeling worthy and valued. I also have a private Facebook group for my team where we recognize their advancements publicly. We post inspirational videos. We do Facebook live posts in there. We continue to paint the picture and share the vision. But the most important thing is to promote and get your team to events. That is where the magic happens. That is where leaders are born. Events don't change your business. They change *you*, which in turn changes your business.

I was already making six figures in my business when I attended my second company event. I hadn't seen the vision yet. I was very successful, but I didn't really see myself as a network marketer. I saw myself as someone who loves these great products, and who just happens to make some really good money by getting into action and telling the world what I was doing. I went to Texas in January of 2014, and an accountant took the stage to share her story. She told us about her two kids (I have two kids!). She told us about her busy life as an accountant (Hey, that's me! Over here!) She told us about having a husband who had a job that didn't serve him. (Were you in my house last week listening to my husband complain for the 1,000,000th time?) I felt like she was talking directly to me. This woman had my story! She had my pain! She was me! Yet I didn't have the belief in network marketing like she did. I just saw it as "extra money" to help with my kids, family, house, etc. Well, after that event, I walked into my boss's office and gave my notice. I was already making three times my annual salary in my full-time and part-time jobs. I knew I could do this. I knew I could make this work. Well, technically, it *was* working, but I was ready! I was ready to be a network marketing professional! That is why getting your team to events is not only mandatory but should be a non-negotiable for anyone who is committed and serious about building a business. You also can't ask your team to do what you're not doing. Get your tickets with urgency as if they will sell out the first day and get your team there. That's how you retain a team!

What have been your most successful marketing strategies you have used to grow your business?

The most successful network marketing strategies that have helped grow my business to a seven-figure cumulative business and multiple six figure annual business is social media. I have been using social media to build my business since day one. I have been consistent on what I post each day. Listen, there are a lot of people that do what I do. I want those who are following me to see my passion, my consistency, and to know I am the expert for weight loss, energy, athletic performance, healthy aging, and wealth creation. One of my teammates once said, "No one wants to be your science experiment." Stay consistent, because they are watching, and when they are ready-whether a month later or five years later-you want them to come to you. But once you stop being consistent, they will look for someone else who can solve their problem.

I also believe in launch parties and get-togethers so you can introduce your product or service to your friends and family or even strangers, all in one place. They can see your passion. They can see your commitment. Give them a safe place to feel there is no pressure. You are the tour guide, the educator, the informant who is giving them information to make an educated decision. Make it fun. Share stories. Have samples. This has been one of the most effective strategies for me as well. I launched my business by having my first meeting at my home. I had almost forty people! Mind you, I didn't have a huge house. People were sitting on each other's laps, on stairs, and even on the floor! But we made it work, and we helped a dozen people change their lives that night.

What three resources do you feel anyone in network marketing needs? Why?

One is a planner for sure! You can't do this business without organization and structure. Planning out your week or even your year in advance is so important. Log in every call and event, personal or business. I use the Passion Planner, which has been the only planner to work for me. Find a planner that works for you and commit to planning out the next day before you go to bed. As your business grows, it may be the next week you plan out, but start by getting a planner and logging in everything. Start with your non-negotiables (church, work, gym, kids' sporting event, etc.), then fill in the blanks.

Creating a duplicatable system for your team to follow is also needed in network marketing. It's a team effort, but it is only going to work if you have something that you can duplicate. Eric Worre says, "People are not duplicatable, systems are." You want someone that you are talking to about the business to say, "I can do that, too," but if you make it complicated, become an ingredient expert, or talk too much instead of guiding someone to a website or a video, you are not duplicating yourself, and that will create chaos.

Contact lists are probably the most important. Without a list, you don't have a business. Having a place to put all your contacts is even more important. Whether it be in an email list or in Excel, putting all your contacts in one place for you to not only keep notes, but easily access them is important. For example, you may have spoken to someone two years ago and forgot, but one day you see that person at the store and they are using your product! Say what? After you stop looking shocked, you ask them how they got started and they tell you they heard about someone at work's sister's mother's cousin doing it. If you forget who you talk to and don't have good notes on them, you will lose them when they are finally ready to join.

How do you keep yourself motivated and encouraged when things don't go right?

I don't have to keep myself motivated. I have to keep myself inspired! Motivation is a tough word. You can be motivated to do things or not motivated, but when you are inspired, you'll do it even when you are not motivated. Waking up with intentions and going to bed with gratitude are extremely important to me. There are times we all get up on that wrong side of the bed. Maybe we didn't sleep well, someone was sick, or we just didn't feel like doing anything that day. It has happened to all of us. Opening your eyes and saying affirmations out loud to start your morning will set the day on the right path. If we get up aggravated, our day will be full of aggravation. If we start our day sad, most of our day will be spent depressed. Priming and meditating are both ways to get your day started off on a positive note, but even that won't motivate me. To be motivated, I need to be inspired, and to be inspired I need to tell myself affirmations over and over that I believe to be true.

I believe in spending at least twenty minutes a day on personal development. Working on yourself is just so important in this business. Podcasts or motivational CD's are great. Sometimes, it takes a change of state or environment to motivate me. I start in my office on some days, and then end up in the kitchen. Or maybe at other times I close the computer, get out the YouTube, and blast my favorite song as I dance wildly around the house.

This all helps, again, not just to motivate me, but to inspire me to keep going even when it's really hard at times.

What advice would you give to a woman entrepreneur who is ready to take her business to the next level?

The advice I would give is: Go for it! That woman deserves this. She deserves to live a life she designed. One where she can do and be her best. Where she can change the world. Live in freedom- financially, with time, in spirit-whatever freedom means to that person.

But I would also tell her that it's going to be hard. It's going to be tough. She may have to make sacrifices. Those sacrifices may be family members, children, friends. If you do what's easy in life, life will eventually get hard, but if you do what's hard in life, life will eventually get easy.

Put your seatbelt on, start your engine, and keep your foot on the gas. This ride is bumpy. It has a lot of turns and even some boulders that will fall in front of you. Keep on track. Don't veer off. Don't try to shortcut it. Keep on the path. Listen to the GPS. It will reroute you when needed. This business is hard. But it is so worth it. I would tell her *she* is so worth it. Just don't quit. Keep moving, because you will be forever grateful for the long-term results instead of focusing on the short-term gain.

What are your insights about the direct selling/network marketing industry that will help women who are growing their own independent consultant businesses?

Treat your business like a business from day one. We have the keys to a million-dollar business, yet so many people treat it like a hobby. Treating it like a business will pay you like a business. I believe when people treat it like a hobby, they quit. Most of the people who become your very first business partners will not be there three years later. Most quit right before they have that breakthrough. Why? Because it got hard. Because they had to choose between this or that. Because someone told them "no." Because their family told them they were nuts. Well, maybe we are, but be proud of being a network marketing professional. Celebrate those "no's." Work on yourself daily. We all get to pick our hard. What's harder? Going to a job that doesn't serve you, or calling a friend to share what you're doing? What's harder? Missing every holiday party at your kid's school because you can't get off work, or going to a network event to meet strangers?

Success will take longer than expected, but where are you going anyway? I hear all the time: "What will your life be like when you are making x amount of money?" or "How will it feel when you can pay off your mortgage?" I ask my new business partners: "What will it feel like when you do nothing different? Where will your life be in six months to a year if you stay exactly where you are?" Showing the pain to someone is more powerful than showing the reward.

We as women take care of everyone before we take care of us. This business gives us a community and culture to feel loved, appreciated, and valued with no cap on the income we can create. We can still take care of others while also taking care of us. As we help others, we help ourselves.

You will have to enroll a lot of people. Get out there and start talking to everyone you know and everyone you meet. You will have to put in the time. You will have to put in the effort. But what can happen in two-to-five years with commitment, hard work, determination, consistency, and perseverance will make all the sweat and tears so worth it.

What book(s) would you recommend to women who are starting their own businesses?

Go Pro by Eric Worre as I mentioned above. I would purchase ten at a time and give them to your new distributors.

You Are a Bad Ass by Jen Sincero is one bad ass book! It teaches you how to stop doubting your greatness and start living an awesome life.

Ice Breakers by Tom "Big Al" Schreiter teaches you in an easy read how to get any prospect to beg you for a presentation.

The Business of the 21st Century by Robert Kiyosaki talks about why network marketing is such a powerful business model. It talks about network marketing, leverage, and residual income. All things most people who get started in network marketing don't know the meaning of.

Learn more about Dawn Ferrentino

Dawn grew up in West Orange, NJ as a middle child of an older sister, Chris, and a younger brother, Mark. Dawn graduated from Montclair State University with honors in 1990. She left with a bachelor's degree in accounting and started her career in public accounting at a large CPA firm performing outside audits. She worked in the corporate world for 27 years. She started in public accounting before moving into the private sector.

Dawn has created a multiple six-figure annual income and is millionaire #175 in Isagenix. She has earned the shooting star and rising star awards on numerous occasions and has been one of the top 120 income earners for the past 5 years. She has earned her way as a Top Achiever 4 years in a row with Isagenix and has been featured on many podcasts, both international and national.

During Dawn's transformation as a product user, she decided everyone deserved to feel as good as she did and design the life they so deserve. Dawn is passionate about health, fitness and freedom, and assists others on creating and designing optimal health and wealth through their own transformations, through both mind and body.

She is also passionate about creating and designing life on your own terms. As a successful entrepreneur, Dawn assists others on how to create financial, time, and physical freedom. Her mission is "To Free Everyone She meets both physically and financially and to Bring All Moms Home from the Work Force to Raise Their Own Children." She has coached, inspired, and motivated thousands of people and helped transform their lives. She is a motivational speaker, coach, entrepreneur, professional network marketer, mentor, trainer and author. She inspires, motivates, and empowers others to be the best they can be. She carries a bachelor's degree in accounting which assists her as a business owner.

As a personal note, Dawn loves the beach, fishing and just being outdoors. She loves a long walk and enjoys watching sunsets.

Living Healthy Naturally, LLC

It's a new day, it's a new dawn, it's a new you!
908-208-0002

Dawnferrentino07@gmail.com
www.dawnferrentino.com
www.dawnferretino.isagenix.com

**No matter what people tell you, words and ideas can change the world.
- Robin Williams**

YOUR NOTES

Made in the USA
Middletown, DE
21 June 2018